KU-731-299

WRITTLE AGRICULTURAL COLLEGE
Department of Extra Mural Studies
LIBRARY CENTRE

WRITTLE AGRICULTURAL COLLEGE
LIBRARY

WITHDRAWN FROM STOCK

3 3012 00027 6111

E 006959792 2 001

Foliage Plants

Frederick A. Boddy

FOLIAGE PLANTS

	The Library Writtle Agricultural College Nr. Chelmsford, Essex	
Copy B	Accessions No. WAC 14204	
	Class No. 635.975	

David & Charles
Newton Abbot

635.975   BV90412

0 7153 5692 5

© Frederick A. Boddy, 1973

All rights reserved. No part of this publication may be
reproduced, stored in a retrieval system, or transmitted,
in any form or by any means, electronic, mechanical,
photocopying, recording or otherwise, without the prior
permission of David & Charles (Holdings) Limited

Set in 12/13 point Perpetua by
C. E. Dawkins (Typesetters) Limited
and printed in Great Britain by
Straker Brothers Limited Whitstable for
David & Charles (Holdings) Limited
South Devon House Newton Abbot Devon

To my wife, Joyce,
who, with patience and understanding,
sits in silence when my pen is at work.

Contents

List of illustrations

Introduction

No garden would be complete without flowers but they are, in the life span of a plant, a purposeful, if fleeting, phase intended for the perpetuation and increase of its kind. A flower without foliage is rather like a picture without a frame—the foliage is the setting which displays the beauty of the flower, preceding it and remaining when that beauty has faded, carrying on with its vital function of providing and maintaining supplies so that the plant as a whole can live, grow and produce progeny.

We, who love gardens, can all appreciate how much we owe to foliage. A garden of flowers without it is unthinkable for then the colour and interest would wane, but a garden of foliage alone, and a most delightful one too, is more than a possibility.

But it was not in that vein that I set out to write this book; rather that I felt the vision is too often dazzled by the flowers. Foliage is not only a necessity for their proper display in that, like the frame, it can add to the picture, but it can, by proper and perhaps subtle use, tone down any harsh lines. Equally as important, it is there for the whole of the growing season and, if of an evergreen nature, for the winter months also when its value is immeasurably increased.

Sometimes foliage takes on the appearance, but not the functions, of the flowers, ie the highly coloured bracts of the popular poinsettia. More often it merely forsakes its natural green for other tones or admixtures of colour, which may be fixed or no more than a passing phase.

Then there is shape and majesty in the broad outlines of a plant influenced as much by the foliage as the stems and branches. Individually, leaves may have quality and texture, be architectural in shape or majestic in proportions. But enough, ere I impinge upon what is to follow! So wide is the

scope with foliage that one could fill several volumes in pro-
claiming its variety, merits and uses. I have, therefore, had
to be content with confining my thoughts to the plants I know
best, concentrating on those which can be used in the small
as well as the larger garden and landscape and, equally as
important, are not so rare as to be beyond the reach of the
majority.

In the compiling of the following chapters there have been
many occasions when I have had difficulty in deciding where
to place some of the subjects. On which side of the boundary
should one put a silvery-grey or a grey-green, and should I
extol a plant primarily for the colour or the form and texture
of its foliage?

Inevitably there have been subjects which do not click into
place. Take the rhododendrons for example. I would not
attempt to analyse the variations in foliage hue but those who
have a deep seated interest will appreciate that having passed
out of glorious floral array they are not necessarily dull green
bushes for the rest of the year.

Of necessity some chapters are by no means as all embracing
as I would have liked, but where does one stop when outlining
the virtues of the inestimable conifers or the innumerable
trees and shrubs which ensure that summer bows out in a
blaze of colour as autumn takes over?

No garden, great or small, can fail to benefit from as much
thought being given to the use of foliage as to its adornment
with flowers, particularly from the season of mists and mellow
fruitfulness to the days when life again springs eternal from
the gradually warming earth. It then serves as more than a
memory to the flowers that have gone, imparting life and
warmth to the garden and landscape when winter wears a
frown.

CHAPTER ONE

Unfurling Leaves

SPRING IS THE season when most plant life begins or starts anew and, as with life generally, youth is clean and fresh and teeming with interest and promise. New young shoots, new leaves, even of the most obnoxious weeds, have a freshness which often belies the character which develops as they pass gradually to puberty, then prime and old age. With most plants the young leaves are at first lighter in colour than normal and thus form the main kaleidoscope of spring, exemplified by the larches in particular. Others depart wholly or partially from anything approaching normal green and assume tints of red, bronze and yellow reminiscent of, but by no means so pronounced as, the glories of autumn days. By and large, of course, youthful freshness and tenderness is but fleeting so, with a few notable exceptions, one would hardly advocate planting for spring foliage effect as one can for the autumn for, unlike the fall, there is a wealth of floral colour to compete with and first catch the eye. But it is true to say that even spring foliage can be used deliberately to enhance spring flowers and to form happy associations and, other things being equal, this is something which should be remembered when selecting plant material for a permanent setting.

Light, fresh, green, unfurling leaves naturally predominate.

Some may stand out more than others as, for instance, the large but still baby-like in proportion, shiny leaves of *Lysichitum americanum* and *L. camtschatcense*, for these are first brought into the distant picture by the equally large spathes, yellow and white respectively, which house the true flowers and which will later be submerged by the foliage as it attains quite massive proportions. *Lysichitum* is a notable plant for the margins of lakes and large pools, the streamside or wet ditch. Or it could be the very light, almost yellowish, green and tapering young foliage of the day lilies, *Hemerocallis*, or of irises like *laevigata*. Wherever ferns unroll their fronds they portray the freshness of youth, extremely delicate with those of finer proportions like that dainty maidenhair, *Adiantum venustum*, or the 'Proliferum' and 'Plumoso-divisilobum' forms of the soft shield fern, *Polystichum setiferum*. Many, like the royal fern, *Osmunda regalis*, precede their unfurling proper with a conspicuous show of brown 'wool' on the back of the rolled fronds. One could quote many other instances of outstandingly fresh, green, young foliage but let us rather take a look at more pronounced colour variations.

Coloured Tips

Little reddish-salmon 'stars' twinkle at the end of every growth of *Erica* 'Dawn' and *Calluna vulgaris* 'Winter Chocolate' as they prepare to commence their seasonal expansion. Coloured tips are also a feature of several cultivars of the Dorset heath, *Erica ciliaris*, and the crossed-leaved heath, *E. tetralix*, which are the parents of the foregoing and several other summer-flowering hybrids. Those of *E. ciliaris* 'Wych' are yellowish green while at the other end of the scale those of 'C. H. Gill' are purplish. So, too, are those of *E. tetralix* 'Con Underwood' with 'Alba Mollis' silver against the grey, adult foliage, which in itself is a feature of many cultivars of the crossed-leaved heath.

Among the tree heaths *E. arborea* 'Gold Tips', as its name

implies, has light-golden, young leaves which form a most
pleasing contrast with its white flowers produced concurrently. *Calluna vulgaris* 'Multicolor', as a prelude to its
summer coat in shades of bronze, orange and yellow, exhibits
promise of things to come with orange-red tips as growth
commences.

The stonecrop, *Sedum acre*, pretty though it may be when
covered with a haze of golden flowers, soon assumes epidemic
proportions as it spreads sideways and often some distance
beyond. Every little piece of its brittle growth broken off
by divers means and dispersed is likely to take root whatever the ground it falls upon. But despite all this a corner
should be found somewhere among the rocks, or even on the
verge of a gravel path, for *S.a.* 'Aureum' whose new growths
start as pale yellow tips, making a glowing patch.

Golden Young Leaves

Apart from those trees and shrubs which clothe themselves
with gold throughout the season, generally more vivid in
youth and with some gradually becoming yellowish green as
the summer advances, there are several whose young foliage
only is golden and turns completely green as it attains full
size.

Euonymus fortunei (*radicans*) 'Variegatus' starts off the season
in yellowish tone before lapsing to its normal silver variegation.
Most conspicuous of all are two trees where not only the
earliest spring leaves are so coloured but there is a con-
tinuation so long as growth continues, often with another
display when a burst of secondary growth occurs around
July, by which time the oldest leaves are at their darkest
green and there is a most delightful contrast as sprigs of golden
green sit on them. *Gleditsia triacanthos* 'Sunburst' is so outstanding in this respect, carrying on in this way for much of
the summer, that it has claims to be called a golden-leaved
tree, under which heading it receives full appraisal later.

Acer cappadocicum (colchicum) 'Aureum' also charms in this way although it does have spells when less golden young growth is evident, while *Sorbus aucuparia* 'Dirkenii' slowly merges into green and becomes completely so when young growth ceases and stems and leaves mature.

Suffusions of Red and Maroon

Of all young foliage which completely departs from its adult green there is none so widely marvelled at and spell binding in its sheer vivacity as the rich scarlet of *Pieris formosa forrestii* and its forms, which only the leaf-like bracts of poinsettias can match for flower-like brilliance. Proof of its captivation are the attempts which have been made to further increase the intensity of colour, as with 'Wakehurst'; while for the purported hybrid with *P. japonica* called 'Forest Flame' the claim, not without justification, is that it is hardier than *forrestii* and later to come into leaf, thus has a better chance of escaping spring frosts which all too often blacken the brilliance overnight.

The other fly in the ointment is that *Pieris* is a lime hater and thus may be barred to those who garden in alkalinity. Soil conditions, if not too much on the adverse side, can often be overcome by some extra ground preparation and it may be possible to avoid frost pockets and sites open to early morning sunshine which play a major part in late spring frost damage.

This spring foliage brilliance is but a corollary in that the white lily-of-the-valley-like flowers are freely produced in conjunction, gracing the shrub before and after the flaming young growths have matured to green.

Reddish-maroon to compete for a time with the summer permanence of purple plums, *Berberis thunbergii atropurpurea* and the like is provided by the young growths of many of the paeonies. *Paeonia cambessedesii* and other species and many of the hybrids emerge with barely a semblance of green while *P. suffruticosa*, the Moutan paeony, is heavily impregnated with bronze-maroon and covered with a greyish bloom.

There is a parallel in deep, rich colour in the first foliage of beds of many of the ever popular hybrid tea and floribunda roses, especially where subjected to fairly severe pruning, but these patches of spring colour are not often singled out for special mention. Some of the garden astilbes, now grouped under *A.* x *arendsii*, can be equally as impressive for a time with the deepest, most uniform colour to be found mainly among those cultivars like 'Fanal', possibly the most colourful of all, 'Granat', 'William Reeves' and others which later produce the deepest red flowers. Others may simply be burnished with varying degrees of red or bronze, the re-mainder differing but little from customary fresh green. So where these delightfully graceful and colourful flowering plants are grown in the moist soil conditions they like, as a prelude to that varied floral display there can be a rehearsal with spring foliage.

Japanese maples with habitual red foliage naturally also contribute their share to the spring scene, augmented by those whose young leaves are tinted with red before de-veloping their natural green. The sharply pointed lobes of the young leaves of *Acer palmatum* hang down like claws before finally unfurling, each tipped and edged with red. *A.p. heptalobum* (*septemlobum*) is also suffused with red and retains its brilliant scarlet bud scales while the leaves are going through the process of unfurling. For more positive and pro-longed effect one of the finest for spring garments is the form of the Norway maple called *A. platanoides* 'Schwedleri' with bright, deep red young leaves and stems which gradually change to their summer coat of green.

The common maple of the hedgerows, *A. campestre*, exhibits a lot of red in the leaves and young growths and in this respect is especially pretty when used for forming a tall hedge, for which purpose it is all too seldom employed. One sees it as a component of country hedges not to be bypassed without an

admiring glance when soft midsummer growths, more likely
to be evident if the hedge has had an early trimming, are a
glowing reddish-pink. This phenomenon occurs also with the
copper beech when employed as a hedge, a somewhat dull
feature if planted in length but admirable when mixed with
the ordinary green. Many young growths encouraged by early
clipping will start off in similar vein, so it is well worthwhile
with both subjects to get in early with the shears and have the
pleasure for a time of these little splashes of bright colour on
a darker background.

A. *cappadocicum* 'Rubrum' with red, young foliage set
against the green of the fully developed leaves behaves in the
same manner as its close relative 'Aureum' and is, on the
whole, a much easier tree to procure and to grow to a good
specimen. That most popular Japanese cherry, *Prunus serrulata*
'Kanzan', so often still erroneously called 'Sekiyama' or
'Hizakura' and so plentifully employed, often in the wrong
situations, in cities and towns, is also notable for the richness
of its bronzed, young leaves. This is also a feature of other
flowering cherries but few have it to the degree presented by
'Kanzan'.

The magnificence of the foliage of the giant rhubarbs is for
another chapter but here *Rheum australe* (*R. emodi*) is worthy
of mention for the great, unfurling leaves and their leaf stalks
may be an intense reddish-maroon. The indecision is because
I have seen this species planted in quantity but not all plants
displaying this intense early coloration although in the same
stage of growth and growing in similar circumstances.

Burnished with Reddish-bronze and Copper

The horse chestnuts are not trees for any but the largest of
gardens and for the landscape. Usually they are represented
by the horse chestnut itself, *Aesculus hippocastanum*, or the red
horse chestnut, *A.* x *carnea*, and they are both magnificent trees
at any time of the growing season. Their fresh green, young

leaves are among the first to be put forth, soon followed by the beautiful, upright panicles of flowers almost exotic in appearance, but neither can quite equal the Indian horse chestnut, *A. indica*, in the radiance of the young leaves which are burnished and streaked with reddish-bronze. This is a tree equal in many respects to the more popular species but, sadly, very much neglected.

So too is the dwarf buckeye, *A. parviflora*, which makes a fine suckering shrub eventually up to 8ft high and by slow sideways spread as much if not more across. Apart from the bronzy tints of spring this shrub has foliage character throughout the summer and waits until July and August before producing its large upright panicles of white flowers, a most conspicuous feature at a season when flowers on shrubs are beginning to get somewhat sparse. It should be much more widely employed, preferably as an isolated specimen in not too cultivated surrounds where it will do itself more justice than hemmed in in a shrub border.

The amelanchiers too have their brief moments with bronzy tints preceding and then linking up with their prolific white blossoms, but their crowning glory is, of course, the autumn. Of quite modest proportions, their dual display makes them well nigh indispensable for the average to fairly small garden. *Cercidiphyllum japonicum* has few peers at leaf fall. It has no floral beauty but in the spring it too is attractively bronze-tinted. There is a fascination in the short spurs each carrying a single leaf to take the foliage right into the branches, even of quite large trees—and it does eventually make a tree of considerable proportions, of graceful appearance and with elegant foliage. *Sorbus hupehensis* likewise is always a feature in the autumn with foliage and white fruits and also is well burnished with bronze in the spring.

Viburnum farreri (*V. fragrans*) and *V.* x *bodnantense* have bronzy young foliage to follow their sweet-scented winter flowers but the pick of the bunch for spring foliage variation is *V. setigerum* (*V. theiferum*) whose leaves were, and may still be, used in a certain monastery for tea making, hence the now deposed specific epithet of *theiferum*, implying a likening to *Thea sinensis*, the shrub whose leaves provide us with tea and which now is officially known as *Camellia sinensis*. *Viburnum setigerum* starts off the season with young leaves which at first are almost wholly reddish-bronze in colour, passing later to green and then to very deep, almost orange yellow. White flowers and fruits which pass from yellow to red make this a shrub of many virtues but one which is, strangely enough, seldom seen outside collections.

Stranvaesia davidiana, a tall, rather-straggling evergreen shrub or small tree, has the unusual habit of allowing some of its foliage to turn to a bright red in autumn as if to emulate the brilliance of deciduous companions, but these are retained throughout the winter along with the usually plentiful crop of rosy-crimson fruits. These do not appear to be palatable to birds and may still be well in evidence when spring growth starts with reddish-bronze young leaves.

So many people think and speak of azaleas only for the sheer brilliance of their flowers. It is well to bear in mind that many of the deciduous cultivars are attractive also with their bronze tinted young foliage, some of the best in this respect to be found in the Exbury and Knaphill group of hybrids, among which 'Basilisk' is quite outstanding.

Several of the honeysuckles provide spring foliage coloration. Notable among these is *Lonicera* x *tellmanniana* whose large coppery-red flowers are among the finest in the genus but, sad to say, scentless. One of its parents, *L. tragophylla*, is even more outstanding in flower and also scentless, with spring foliage of even deeper hue. *Clematis montana rubens* begins with a pronounced infusion of red in the young leaves and stems before it clothes itself with a profusion of blooms.

Those magnificent foliage plants *Rodgersia pinnata* and *R. podophylla*, thrust up fully bronze unfurling leaves and before

Rodgersia podophylla: large, deeply divided leaves which impart character to the woodland and waterside throughout the summer.

they become completely green the great ovate leaves of
Cardiocrinum giganteum (*Lilium giganteum*) have a deep bronze
fanning outwards from the base to the mid-rib until it merges
into green.

The epimediums are redoubtable ground coverers for
partially shaded places, always tidy and always attractive. They
are best cut back as soon as spring activity is about to start, the
evergreen species then having done their job of clothing the
ground with most acceptable foliage. This makes way for the
young foliage which may be a delightful light green or
delicately permeated with bronze. Cutting back also permits
their charming little spurred flowers, so reminiscent of
aquilegias or columbines, in shades of yellow, cream, white,
crimson, coppery-red or pink, to be better seen and appreciated. *Epimedium* x *versicolor*, *E.* x *rubrum* and *E. grandiflorum*
'Lilacinum' are among the finest for tinted spring foliage.

Silver above and below

Just as ordinary green leaves are generally much lighter and
brighter than those which have attained full size and maturity
so too with those which have permanent silver or silvery-grey
foliage, rather like freshly minted coins among those which
have become somewhat tarnished with age. Then some plants
confine their silver to the undersides of the leaves where it is
rather less obvious and as if to make amends may attempt to
display it more openly and at its brightest before the leaves
completely unfurl and assume their normal plane. This is so
with some of the taller large-leaved cotoneasters of *C. frigidus*
type, *C.* 'Cornubia' in particular. But for sheer silvery whiteness in immaturity there is nothing to beat the *Sorbus* of the
whitebeam group, *S. aria* itself growing in the wild on a
chalky hillside where it is completely at home, with the greens
of other trees for a backcloth. It will stand out in quite
startling contrast and be seen for miles.

Malus tschonoskii, so valuable for pyramidal form and autumn foliage, has a distinct silvery sheen for a time when its new leafage is being unfolded. Others which start the season in like manner all contribute to the effectiveness of the spring panorama.

Multi-shades in Foliage

One of the most delightful of all trees for spring foliage is a form of the common sycamore, *Acer pseudoplatanus* 'Brilliant-issimum'. At first this is an exquisite shade of coral-pink with a hint of cream, then gradually changes to yellowish-green diffused with darker coloration until, after a week or so of its charms, its final tone of light, striated green is reached. This tree expands slowly and somewhat laboriously and although it may, after many, many years, attain a stature and a spread of some 20ft or so, on account of its very limited rate of growth, it is essentially a tree for the small garden for it is hardly likely to exert any dominance in a lifetime. Indeed, it could profitably be grown in bush form as an associate with, or substitute for, the Japanese maples. A chance seedling, apparently from the sycamore itself, catching the eye because of its pinkish seed leaves, was potted up out of curiosity and I now have a delightful small bush in its 'teens and still no more than 2ft in height. It is more or less identical with 'Brilliant-issimum' in its foliage. In its thirteenth year, as if to be capricious, it produced an extra strong growth with leaves like the variegated sycamore, 'Leopoldii'. This was no asset to the bush and was quickly removed. Used in association with a bank of heathers this miniature is always an object of admiration in the spring and around July it sometimes decides to make a little secondary growth which is even more colour-ful than the first for it usually starts off a brilliant salmon-red before passing through the normal colour phases.

   A. pseudoplatanus 'Prinz Handjery' is another sycamore with somewhat similar foliage but I do not know it well enough to recount any differences in leaf coloration or rate of growth.

A. negundo 'Elegans' ('Elegantissimum') shows some staining of pink in the young, golden variegated leaves and this colour also creeps into *Glechoma hederacea* 'Variegata' and that excellent waterside grass, *Glyceria maxima* 'Variegata'.

It is to be regretted, of course, that the pure freshness, the pastel coloration or, on the other hand, the ruddiness of youth, in short the budding joys of spring, cannot be more prolonged for all too quickly it commences to pass to the teenage state and adult status and then old age begins to creep in as summer passes to its zenith. But what of it? The seasons come and go and each in turn brings its own particular brand of interest, of joy and inspiration and a poor gardener is he who does not derive pleasure from his efforts and his picture at any time of the year, whilst looking forward with anticipation to what is in store as the seasons and the years roll relentlessly by. If he does really appreciate foliage as well as flowers, and plants accordingly, he can be certain there will always be something to please and strike a chord.

CHAPTER TWO

Shades of Green
Throughout the Year

As JUNE DAWNS the varied tints of spring begin to settle down into the regular pattern of summer and we are then inclined to take the general green coat of plant life very much for granted. When it is desired to introduce foliage colour variation we all too often think in terms of gold, silver and purple or maroon, in whole or as a variegated component and are apt to forget that subtle variations of the many different hues of plant greens contribute most towards ensuring that the predominating colour of the landscape remains soothing to the eye, never glaring and never boring. It is, perhaps, only when we encounter acre after acre, mile after mile, of block planting of pines and other dark green conifers for timber production that we realise just how much the natural blends of green mean to the world of nature.

Even when we intermingle plant life mainly with the aim of floral colour, and perhaps form, there is seldom any violent lack of harmony in the green foliage which is thrown together in juxtaposition; it is only when one compares the heterogeneous mass, or sees it side by side, with an association in which thought has been given to the choice and the blending of the greens as well as other colours that one realises just how much more can be achieved. How often we see a dark corner made all the more gloomy because it is dominated by foliage of sombre tone which could be better employed as a background or as a foil upon which to display the dazzling lighter tones of flowers.

It takes a first class artist with first class painting materials to reproduce faithfully the many and varied shades of green in the plant life around us. To analyse and break these down is altogether too complicated and, indeed, rather unnecessary. It is, perhaps, the extremes which need segregating from the mass—the very light and the very dark greens, the grey-greens and particularly those of shining texture which have the greatest impact. I shall, therefore, only attempt to pick out a few which can be arrayed alongside the other more radical variations covered in subsequent chapters, variations whose contribution to the general panorama, although of some consequence, is but incidental to the basic hue.

Light and Bright Greens

We have already noted the light, fresh-green of the infantile foliage of the day lilies, *Hemerocallis*, which deepens but little in tone as it matures and becomes surmounted by the flowers in many delightful and subtle shades and blends. This can be used to good effect in shady corners which these normally sun-loving plants will also furnish with credit. It is here, too, that we can make full and profitable use of *Vancouveria hexandra*, a dainty, clump-forming carpeter so akin to the epimediums in appearance of foliage and flowers that it seems strange it is not one of them. Apart from the flowers which differ slightly in their component parts one can regard it merely as a lighter, more graceful edition of the barrenworts. In all other respects we can accord it the same treatment.

While the shining, light, evergreen leaves of *Pachysandra terminalis* may often give way to the variegated form it is really a more efficient carpeter in that it is quicker to establish itself and help keep weeds at bay.

Pachysandra terminalis: a popular ground coverer with shining evergreen leaves.

Geranium macrorrhizum will crop up again but let me here extol it, firstly as a ground coverer par excellence and, secondly, for the pleasant light-green of its foliage. *Tellima grandiflora* too will get another hearing but likewise cannot be omitted for its pleasing, rounded, light-green summer foliage, and the hostas deserve commendation all along the line. One of the lightest and brightest of the greens is *H. plantaginea* 'Grandiflora' and there are others somewhat richer but equally as bright in their green tones.

For the woodland border the toad lilies, *Tricyrtis hirta* and *T. macropoda* have most attractive, shining green foliage, and flowers, white and yellow respectively, exquisitely spotted with purple and with a prominent style terminated by three large reflexing stigmas. Like so many shade lovers, their flowers are full of charm and character at close quarters rather than bright and conspicuous at some distance away.

Kirengeshoma palmata from Japan may be planted largely for the charm of its nodding bell-shaped, soft-yellow flowers but while one is waiting for these to be produced in the latter half of the summer one can enjoy the arching stems with their light-green, palmately-lobed leaves paling to yellowish-green as the summer advances. Also a lover of shade and moist, well drained, humus-containing soil this is one of the ballerinas of the woodland garden. Here, too, is the place for *Boykinia aconitifolia* with its round, deeply-lobed, light-green leaves which are equally as valuable for bringing relief into the shady place as the crowded corymbs of white flowers on 2-2½ft stems.

When they first appear above ground the arching stems of the false spikenard, *Smilacina racemosa*, can be mistaken for those of the old Solomon's seal, *Polygonatum multiflorum*, but later the relatively slight differences are obvious. Light, fresh green, particularly in tender youth, even when the massed plumes of white flowers, which terminate each stem in spring, have died away the arching stems and leaves have considerable value for the whole of the summer. While it may prefer a cool, damp soil it is not a choosey plant and I have it growing with comparative disdain in competition with the avid surface roots of silver birches.

The meadow saffron, *Colchicum* spp., is one of those comparatively few hardy ground plants which are oddities in that their flowers and foliage are not produced concurrently. Flowers are put forth in the early autumn from otherwise apparently inactive corms, then all seemingly goes to rest for the winter until, quite early in spring, up come the large linear-lanceolate, bright-green leaves to give much freshness and character until they start to decline in late June.

Tiarella cordifolia has few peers as a close growing, fairly short, ground coverer in sun or shade with attractive light-green summer foliage burnishing in the winter. *T. wherryi* and *T. trifoliata* have similar foliage and floral qualities but, unlike *cordifolia* which is stoloniferous, are clump formers and do not make a solid mat quite so speedily.

Rubus fockeanus of gardens is a prostrate unarmed bramble which thrusts its stems along the ground, rooting at the nodes and soon forming a dense low mat of bright-green, crinkled leaves set off by the reddish-brown hue of the leaf stalks and top side of the decumbent stems. The flowers are sparingly produced and have no great value. For clothing ground beneath trees and any sort of dry or moist, sunny or gloomy place this is a first class evergreen carpeter which only needs a little checking when it reaches the boundary of its allotted territory. *R. odoratus*, on the other hand, is a fairly tall, also unarmed, shrub of considerable floral beauty but here we mention it for its light, fresh-green foliage and its capacity to thrive under trees.

Shady places can, of course, always be well and attractively clothed with ferns, almost without exception providing an airy, fresh light to dark-green mantle. The evergreen polystichums, *Phyllitis*, and blechnums are especially valuable. So too are the bamboos like *Arundinaria* (*Sinoarundinaria*) *murieliae* and *Phyllostachys flexuosa* which, throughout the year in sun or shade, will provide pleasant greenery or background.

The sarcococcas are invaluable dwarf shrubs planted primarily for their ability to form a shrubby ground cover in shady places and for their sweetly fragrant, if rather inconspicuous, winter flowers. Generally they have a pleasant, dark, shining-green foliage but plant the commonest and dwarfest species, *S. humilis*, where it gets some measure of sunlight but not so much as to make it unhappy, and its foliage will assume quite an inviting yellowish sheen.

The skimmias, be they *S. japonica* and its sexual variants, *S. reevesiana* (*S. fortunei*) or *S. japonica* 'Rubella', most acceptable for their sweetly scented flowers and long lasting fruits, are pleasantly bright-green compact shrubs during the summer, acquiring a deeper tone as their foliage matures. They are subjects for sun or shade, clear or polluted air and *S. japonica* itself is equally at home in limy and acid soils. *S. reevesiana*, on the other hand, dislikes alkaline conditions.

Griselinia littoralis has shiny, apple-green foliage and is an excellent evergreen for maritime conditions. Being a New Zealander there are qualifications as to suitability for colder areas but I have found it to be perfectly hardy and amiable and a most useful stand-by in the smoke besmirched conditions of industrial Lancashire.

The common broom, *Cytisus* (*Sarothamnus*) *scoparius*, and its numerous cultivars is always a bright, fresh, green in stem and foliage. *Hebe subalpina* is one of several of its race which are permanent foliar assets. This has exceptionally bright, light-green leaves on a compact, dome-shaped plant.

Whatever we may hear, read about or think of the common laurel, *Prunus laurocerasus*, we ought to acknowledge that its light-green, shiny leaves, very formal in outline, can be used to good effect. Forget about its somewhat heavy and portly appearance as a hedge, so often mutilated with shears instead of being cut with secateurs, about its preponderance when used as one of the occupants, eventually assuming a dominant role, in an ill-planned shrub border. Think of it rather as a subject which will constitute an evergreen background in sun or shade, any soil or situation, will stand cutting back to mere stumps if it gets too cumbersome and grow away again quite unperturbed. As a filler of the place where we do not wish to plant anything select we can praise and not malign it for some of the real value it possesses.

Although it can be planted as a free-standing shrub the winter sweet, *Chimonanthus praecox* (*C. fragrans*) is more often used to furnish a wall where its sweetly-scented, creamy-yellow flowers suffused with purple in the centre can be visually and nasally appreciated when they appear on the leafless branches in the early months of the year. Throughout the summer the light-green, rather luxuriant foliage forms a pleasant cladding for the wall.

At least one true climbing shrub is worth planting for its

Hebe subalpina: neat domes of bright green foliage throughout the year.

bright shining foliage alone. *Celastrus orbiculatus* (*C. articulatus*) resplendent in autumn with its dying foliage and twisted, curling branches wreathed with the fruitfulness of golden-yellow containers opening to reveal scarlet-arilled seeds, has much ornamental value before its hey-day, despite the extreme modesty of its flowers.

By the waterside the light, shining-green of the lysichitums, in the herbaceous border the heleniums and the yellowish-green of *Solidago* 'Lemore' and *Euphorbia epithymoides* (E. *polychroma*)—there is a host of subjects which, if one will only pause to consider, can impart much of the freshness of spring to the garden for the remaining months of the year, whether or not floral beauty and colour goes with it at some period of its existence.

Darker, Sombre Tones

So we take a brief glance at the other end of the colour scale. Sombre means dark and gloomy and we must ensure when using the darker shades of foliage in our plantings that we call a halt when dark threatens to become gloomy. Remember again how funereal are endless belts of pine forest.

There is a place for the more sober tones of green in any garden. One of the dullest is *Olearia haastii*, a shrub which compensates for its daily appearance with a shower of virgin-white flowers in late summer, followed by silvery seed heads and always with the capacity to thrive in any situation, including the salt spray of coastal towns and the smog of industrial areas. No doubt the heavy, green foliage of the common yew, *Taxus baccata*, had something to do with it being planted in countless churchyards and cemeteries. But this density of tone and strength of character can always be harnessed for background effects, for breaking down or show-ing off bright colours. In particular, it is priceless as a back-cloth for the flowers of the winter cherries, *Lonicera fragrant-issima* and its allies, *Hamamelis*, *Cornus mas* and other trees and shrubs which flower on leafless branches.

Camellias somehow escape criticism for theirs is a more shining darkness and they are remembered and appreciated for their showy flowers, in some years barely a passing phase if late frosts take a hand. Nevertheless, I do feel that when planted in depth they are depressing for most of the year, but an odd plant or group will always impart a richness of foliage tone. But perhaps this is because I have never waxed enthusiastic over camellias, largely because I have some aversion to any formal, double flower of waxy appearance, an injustice maybe to the camellias among which are to be found many with more graceful single or semi-double flowers.

Green hollies are inseparable from both the country and the garden scene. Use their shiny solidity with care and purpose and avoid phalanxes by breaking up with variegated or coloured foliage of this or some other subject. The holly-like *Osmanthus delayayi* and *O. heterophyllus* (*O. ilicifolius*) with deliciously scented white flowers in spring and autumn respectively, also need employing with discretion. So too does *Phillyrea decora* and x *Osmarea burkwoodii*, the latter a bi-generic hybrid between *Phillyrea* and *Osmanthus delavayi*, both highly desirable glossy, dark-green foliage shrubs, also with very fragrant white flowers in spring.

Perhaps the eternal green privet has lowered *Ligustrum* in the social graces but the genus does contain several species which are quite desirable flowering shrubs. One of the best is *L. lucidum* which, although usually seen as a large shrub does make a most presentable and neat dwarf to medium-sized tree and, being evergreen, although it may lose some of its leaves during a particularly severe winter, could be used much more often to fill a great gap for, conifers apart, good evergreen trees are very, very limited. Moreover, it is excellent for town conditions. Shining, dark green, oval leaves up to 6in long make it a conspicuous and desirable subject, and when the erect terminal panicles of white flowers are put forth in late summer it can be an object of considerable admiration.

The strawberry tree, *Arbutus unedo*, apart from its intriguing habit of producing equally intriguing flowers and strawberry-like fruits together during the winter months, is a first-class evergreen foliage shrub. So too are the viburnums, *V. rhytidophyllum* and the dwarf, dome forming *V. davidii*, today beloved and sometimes over used for shrubby cover. Among the hebes there is much variance in foliage tones from the light green of *H. subalpina* previously mentioned through interminable shades to the darker tones of other species and hybrids, not forgetting the old faithful *H. brachysiphon*, formerly *Veronica traversii* which, although as a flowering shrub it has lost some of its one time popularity to a host of hybrids, still has many uses, even if away from the footlights.

While the dark, evergreen leaves, greyish-green beneath, of *Garrya elliptica* may generally be regarded as the backcloth for the long, greyish, winter catkins they have immense value as a background for other subjects and in their own right, especially when clothing a wall to which this shrub is usually assigned.

Perhaps the majority of people who look with favour upon the Chanticleer pear, *Pyrus calleryana* 'Chanticleer', one of the newer Ed Scanlon introductions, will do so for its white flowers and particularly its close pyramidal habit which makes it a promising recruit for small gardens, narrow streets and other confined places. Those with an eye to foliage verdure will be most attracted by its typical pear-like, glossy-green leaves which are retained well into the winter, a few of which, still green, may well be in evidence when growth recommences.

Also of a green rather deeper than most deciduous trees, *Crataegus* x *lavallei* (*C.* x *carrierii*) too hangs on to its foliage until around Christmas time and even longer to its large orange-scarlet haws. This does make a larger tree than the hawthorn and its double flowered cultivars but is not a particularly fast grower once the exuberance of youth has passed and, unlike the hawthorn, does not respond to pruning with a multiplicity of sap shoots to further complicate the problem of containing it.

Now from the taller, woody, dark-green subjects down to one which will thrive unabashed in the dry shade of trees, even right up to the boles of large elms and birches and at the very foot of privet hedges which normally produce at least a yard of barren soil on either side. By and large the euphorbias are sun lovers but *E. robbiae* seems to take any conditions in its stride. Make no mistake about it, this can be a marauder for it thrusts out slender rhizomes beneath the surface and is capable of sending them beneath paving stones to produce growths on the other side. But all this can be forgiven with a subject which deigns to grow cheerfully in places which are

Euphorbia robbiae: shining evergreen foliage, quite happy in the dry shade of trees.

anathema to most plants, even the majority of shade lovers. The dark, evergreen, glossy foliage concentrated in rosette form towards the ends of the stems has a great deal of character and appeal, added to by the erect flowering panicles which commence to push forth as early as February and whose attraction is the yellowish-green bracts surrounding the inconspicuous flowers.

A miniature in proportion but also capable of forming a dense, low, dark-green mat in the driest and shadiest conditions, *Arisarum* (*Arum*) *proboscideum* is always intriguing to visitors when they are shown the little, long-tailed spathes tucked away beneath the foliage to earn it the name of 'mouse plant'. Unfortunately its period above ground is rather short—like several other shade plants by early August it is ready to call it a day and go to winter rest.

The asarabacca, *Asarum europaeum*, although it has no close botanical affinity, has much similarity in name and in habit except that it likes moister ground. It tucks away its curious brown flowers with three-cleft perianth amidst the mat of rounded, glossy, dark-green leaves and soon creates a dense carpet by the spread of its underground rhizomes.

Seldom accorded a place in gardens but widely used by those who specialise in carpet bedding, the rupture wort, *Herniaria glabra*, is worth a little bouquet for it can be used profitably and effectively as a ground-hugging, glistening, dark-green carpeter in sun or shade, preferably in poor soil. Being an evergreen it makes an admirable, dark base coat for the early dwarf bulbs which need a permanent low blanket to clothe the ground and protect them when they go to summer rest.

Grey-green Foliage

Without transgressing into grey foliage which is due for fuller consideration later, although one finds it hard to determine the border line between the hues, we can here look at a few which have a greyish cast of foliage tone, often due to a glaucous bloom or a coating of short hairs.

The cultivated lady's mantle, *Alchemilla mollis*, is quite superb with foliage hue and character upon which to display the foaming sprays of tiny sulphur-green flowers. The quite large leaves are meticulously rounded and lobed and soft and velvety to the touch. Although this plant tends to be given the role of clump forming ground coverer for sun and shade and faithfully serves its master in this way it ought at times to be planted solely for the foliage character it exudes.

Geranium renardii also tends to play a similar role and likewise is worthy of a more selective assignment. Its leaves are a smaller version of the lady's mantle, attractively reticulated, and there is a delicate appeal in the white flowers lightly veined with purplish-mauve to impart a dove-grey cast which tones in beautifully with the greyish-green, velvety foliage.

Dicentra formosa 'Bountiful' and the newer 'Adrian Bloom' have finely cut glaucous grey-green foliage. Throughout the summer they will seldom be without a few of their pendent

Alchemilla mollis: grey-green velvety foliage making excellent ground cover.

locket-like pink or red flowers after the early flush but are well worth planting for their foliage alone.

Considering it has been in cultivation for well nigh two centuries the Japanese balloon flower, *Platycodon grandiflorus*, ought to be in every garden but, strangely, this is not so although it is by no means a rarity. When one adds glaucous grey-green leaves to its attractions of large cup shaped flowers in blue, white or pink from the middle to the end of summer it is surprising it is not widely used for the front of the herbaceous border.

Here, too, but towards the background for they are much taller than the foot high *Platycodon*, we should not overlook the value of the grey-green foliage of the globe thistle, *Echinops ritro*, of *Thalictrum aquilegiifolium* and of *Baptisia australis*, although they are planted primarily for their flowers. The artistic use of foliage should be an integral part of herbaceous border planning. Too often it gets but scant attention and when this is so those subjects with foliage which, in or out of flower, have character of form and colour have greatly enhanced value. *Thalictrum* and *Baptisia* are three-star plants with flowers, colourful and finely divided foliage.

Sedum spectabile and the hybrid *S*. 'Autumn Joy' ('Herbstfreude') are also three-star border plants with a glaucous-grey bloom to the foliage throughout the summer, leading to a long display of flowers from late summer onwards which turn a most attractive brown for late autumn and winter colour.

The glaucous-green of some of the euphorbias is invaluable. *E. characias* sub-spp. *wulfenii* is a real architectural plant, *E. myrsinites* is a fine trailer for the rock garden and although it can be extremely invasive, if a safe place can be found for it around trees or, conversely, on a sunny, arid bank, there is a lot of pleasure in looking at the cypress spurge, *E. cyparissias*, whose stems are densely set all round with narrow, linear, light-green with a greyish cast leaves reminding one of bottle brushes. In the autumn, unlike the preceding which are ever-

greens, it dies off in a haze of clear yellow. It is also worth
having a few self sown seedlings of the annual caper spurge,
E. *lathyris*, often misspelt *lathyrus*, springing up among other
plants in sun or shade, their long upright stems with opposite
pairs of narrow, 3-4in long leaves in four ranks standing out
like sentinels until they begin to flop about under the weight
of long-stalked umbels of green bracts and inconspicuous
flowers followed by large, three-celled fruits. This is the
plant which is claimed to be effective in driving moles away
from the area, something I have never put to the test.

Most shrubs with grey in their foliage are sufficiently
distinct to be covered under that more precise heading later.
Hebe cupressoides is more definitely grey-green in appearance

Euphorbia characias sub-spp. *wulfenii*: form and foliage make this a plant of
real character.

and is a most unusual shrub, being more cypress-like than hebe-like in foliage, hence its specific name. The leaves are minute and little more than scales and it is really the very much divided branchlets rather than these leaves which give its air of distinction. Like most of the hebes it is a free grower tending after a few years to get rather tall, rank and somewhat bare at the base but, like the rest of its kin, it roots readily from cuttings and can easily be replaced.

For bringing the front of a shrub border or bed down to ground level *Dorycnium hirsutum* is just the thing. This is a sub-shrub whose branches die down to the base each winter and are replaced the following year by 18in high twiggy growths clothed with small, woolly, greyish-green foliage and a profusion of heads of pinkish-white flowers followed by reddish seed pods which afford a ready means of propagation. This useful but not well-known subject also provides a lot of material in foliage, flowers or fruit for the flower arranger.

This chapter is really very incomplete but as I said at the outset I would only touch upon a few extremes. To have attempted to explore the depths of green coloration—and there is no colour more varied in its shades—would have been confusing. Indeed, it has not been easy in a limited way to avoid stepping over border lines but perhaps I have written enough to put the green earth in some form of perspective and to emphasise how, in harnessing nature we can not only emulate her soothing blends but deliberately take advantage of the individual shades of green which are available to us.

CHAPTER THREE

Golden Glitter and Silver Foil

GOLD IS A precious metal not to be bandied about without some discrimination, but there is no dearth of it in a garden for there are golden yellow flowers in abundance. They bring sunshine to the scene at all seasons; in the spring in particular they tend to predominate. To augment with broad splashes of similarly coloured foliage could result in too much glitter and impart a feeling of artificiality and unrest. One must, therefore, introduce such foliage with a deal of discretion, having as one's prime object the need to brighten up other-wise dull places, to enhance the value of subjects of darker tone, to add a little 'sunshine' to the winter months or, maybe, create a contrast at some point which will bring a somewhat distant view into relief.

With winter in mind one's thoughts immediately turn to the numerous golden forms of conifers, which are dealt with separately. By and large these provide most of the winter 'sunshine' for few other evergreens have completely golden foliage and no great number where this tone is a component of variegation. The golden form of the Japanese box, *Buxus microphylla japonica* 'Aurea', can therefore be quite invaluable at that season for its leaves are a clear-cut yellow. There is a decided golden tone suffused with green in the small leaves and young shoots of the compact growing *Hebe ochracea* (*H. armstrongii* of gardens) and the golden heath, *Cassinia fulvida* (*Diplopappus chrysophyllus*). This latter has no real affinity to the heaths except in general appearance although it can be associated with them to impart variety if not for the colour of its foliage, which is more than adequately provided for by the heaths themselves. This subject is apt to get a little leggy and untidy after a year or two but can be kept compact if the longest shoots are shortened back each spring.

A few years ago the great heather family could boast only two or three forms whose foliage was naturally of a golden tone, if not very pronounced. Today there is quite a host of new cultivars with highly coloured foliage, continually being added to and making it difficult to differentiate between all their obvious merits. So far the common ling, *Calluna vulgaris*, has been the most prolific in this respect. If one had to confine one's choice to a few with the cleanest foliage tones and with the added bonus of variety in the colour of their flowers— although these do not always show to the best advantage on such a background—one could select 'Gold Haze' (white flowers), 'Sunset' (pink), 'Late Crimson Gold' (crimson) and 'John F. Letts' (pale mauve) of spreading habit. Then, I suppose, this would not be doing justice to such attractive kinds as 'Golden Carpet', 'Golden Feather', 'Orange Queen' and a host of others.

Some people are a little wary of indulging, if that is the right word, in heaths, fearing that they are bound to languish in their own particular soil, having heard so much about peat and acid conditions being absolutely essential. It is certainly true that among the summer-flowering species, *Erica terminalis* (*E. stricta*) excepted, and *E. vagans* which will tolerate a little lime, any soil which hovers around or above neutral may be anathema. Where alkalinity is not too great it can actually be reduced to a safe level by the simple expedient of adding flowers of sulphur, up to 4oz per sq yd at any one time, thoroughly incorporating with the soil as long as possible before planting. If this amount is found on subsequent test to have failed to bring the Ph down to the required level a further application can be made or, if the plants are then in position, up to 1½oz per sq yd can be worked carefully into the top soil around them.

There is an idea abroad that Sequestrene is the answer but the plain truth is that this substance is rather akin to the pain relieving tablets so often prescribed for human beings in that it merely enables a plant to live with the pains of alkalinity by correcting iron deficiency and needs to be repeated at regular intervals if they are to survive.

The strange thing is that the winter and spring flowering species, cultivars and hybrids, almost without exception, can be planted in soils which are not too heavily impregnated with lime. Summer and winter alike, however, a high humus content in the soil is appreciated and this, if not already present, is best achieved by the liberal incorporation of peat when preparing the ground.

The winter-flowering *Erica carnea* hardly needs to boast foliage forms for it chooses to display its full floral glory at that season. 'Aurea', which has been with us for some time, is at its most golden best in the summer when there is close competition but the newcomer 'Foxhollow', of prostrate habit, enhances its gold with fleckings of salmon-pink and red at the approach of winter. It can thus be an asset where the cultivation of summer-flowering heaths is not practical.

The first golden foliage form of *E. vagans* called 'Valerie Proudley' whose vivid gold tone intensifies and then really lights up the winter days is a decided acquisition. Then there is sure to be a place for the golden forerunner of the taller Irish heaths, *E. mediterranea* 'Golden Dome', which also provides white flowers from February to April and variety of form as a specimen among its dwarfer growing associates.

Deciduous Trees and Shrubs

Among deciduous shrubs there is a fair choice to add to the sunshine of the summer. Many may shudder at the sight of golden privet hedges but acknowledge that this oft-maligned shrub, properly used and treated, still has few peers as a foliage shrub of its hue. Sparingly employed, and in the right situation, and the urge to keep it within bounds with shears duly stifled, it can be quite delightful. Some restriction may well be necessary, although it is far less vigorous than its green counterpart. This should take the form of cutting back the longest growths as often as required, right into the heart of the bush to avoid any semblance of a 'haircut'.

Those who have had a spell practising horticulture in industrial climes may be excused if they tend to lose interest in the golden elder when they move to more congenial pastures to practise their art. Yet in all fairness one has to concede that it has much to commend it, apart from its capacity to thrive, if all too quickly tarnished by sooty deposits, in atmospheres where plant cultivation has many limitations. Of the two commonly grown forms I think that *Sambucus racemosa* 'Plumosa Aurea', with its finely divided leaves, is rather more genteel than *S. nigra* 'Aurea', but that may be a matter of opinion.

Philadelphus coronarius 'Aureus', naturally somewhat less vigorous than the type and making a medium sized shrub only, has a lot of charm with its bright-yellow, spring and early-summer foliage gradually changing to greenish yellow with age. Much the same can be said of the golden flowering currant, *Ribes sanguineum* 'Brocklebankii', which makes a well-coloured dwarf shrub, all the better for a little shade from the mid-day sun as the foliage is rather apt to scorch. Then there is 'Aureum', the golden form of the mountain currant, *R. alpinum*, which is also dwarf and well worthy of inclusion in a garden. Neither should be confused with the golden currant, *R. odoratum* (*R. aureum* of gardens) whose common name is applied to the yellow flowers and not the foliage. This shrub I regard as having no outstanding value, although its flowers are quite sweetly scented.

In somewhat similar vein *Physocarpus opulifolius* 'Luteus' is a good yellow when its leaves are in the young state and the summer may be well on its way before they finally age to a yellowish green. The flowers are white, tinged pink and are followed by pod-like fruits, actually inflated follicles, which are bright red as they split along the seams. The peeling bark in winter exposing the brighter under surface is another feature of this shrub, making it a subject of interest the year round, surprisingly very much neglected in gardens. It is so closely allied to *Spiraea* that it has been known as *S. opulifolia* and it also rejoices in the common name of nine bark, no doubt some reference to its winter characteristic.

Lonicera nitida had its moments of publicity and popularity for hedge making. While it must be acknowledged that it does make a very neat, clipped barrier, interest has waned somewhat because it needs almost as much clipping as the ubiquitous privet, and unless given this periodic attention and kept wider at the base than the apex it tends to become gappy towards ground level. Its form 'Baggeson's Gold' is quite a low-growing shrub with tiny golden leaves, a certain amount of green in the older ones ensuring that it is not quite such an intense, hard gold as golden privet and, altogether, it is quite a pleasing subject for the front of the shrub border or for a low hedge.

Light intensity has an influence on colour tones, particularly that of foliage. Generally a fair measure of sunlight, if not full sun, brings out the best colour. Nature, however, is capricious and we find that the golden barberry, *Berberis thunbergii* 'Aurea', a welcome breakthrough in foliage in this erstwhile genus, gives of its best in light shade. The vivid gold of the early spring of this most promising cultivar is maintained for the longest period under these conditions, otherwise it tends to decrease in intensity as the summer advances.

It is strange that more use is not made of the golden form of the common hop, *Humulus lupulus* 'Aureus', a perfectly good golden foliaged climber which, being herbaceous in character, starting afresh from ground level annually is easier to keep under control. So many vigorous climbers have a habit of becoming a tangled, overgrown mass after a few years unless they can be permitted unrestricted spread, attempts to curb and regulate their growth tending to increase their vigour and may result in some loss of flower.

Turning to trees which bring sunshine to the higher reaches, I often think of a distant view of a single golden poplar, *Populus* x *canadensis serotina* 'Aurea' pleasantly glowing against the rather more sombre background of common elms. It seems a pity that more use is not made of a tree which, sparingly used, could create many similar pictures in the countryside. The untrammelled growth, avaricious roots and susceptibility to bacterial canker of some species has put a kind of stigma on the use of poplars for anything other than commercial and quick screening purposes and certainly they are, generally, not trees for gardens other than those of major proportions.

Of lesser stature but still a little too large for the average-to-small garden, the golden sycamore, *Acer pseudoplatanus* 'Worleei', has quite richly coloured foliage for much of the summer months and this foliage tone is accentuated by the reddish leaf stalks. Of more immediate value for the garden and more intense in colour is the all yellow cultivar of the box elder, *A. negundo* 'Auratum', known also as 'Aureum' and 'Californicum Aureum'. Some shelter from strong winds is desirable as the box elders are rather brittle of growth. With any of the foliage forms one must keep a look-out for the appearance of completely green shoots and remove them before their more vigorous growth asserts domination.

Sorbus aria 'Chrysophylla' is a desirable form of the white-beam and is dwarfer and rather more upright. The upper surfaces of the leaves are a soft gold throughout the summer. This is a tree worthy of much more acknowledgement than it seems to be accorded.

Capable of ultimately making quite a respectable sized tree though rather less widespread than its parent, the golden Indian bean tree, *Catalpa bignonioides* 'Aurea', has equally large leaves and is of a positive unfading colour making it a subject of considerable character and value, used to best effect as an individual specimen against a darker background.

Robinia pseudacacia 'Frisia', like golden privet hedges, if too liberally employed could become somewhat loud and vulgar, but an odd tree, carefully sited to catch the eye and no more, can be a fair contributor in a garden rather than a major land-scape scene. Like the false acacia itself there is some lushness of growth in the flush of youth and a tendency towards brittleness but this, I feel sure, could be corrected by a rigorous annual pruning for the first few years to build up a solid, divided basal framework. Indeed, there seems no reason why a feathered tree should not be converted by annual pruning into a trained pyramidal specimen for a small garden, valuable alike for its contour and its rich-golden foliage; but one rather rebels against the thought of applying fruit tree discipline to an ornamental tree with a natural, pleasing, rounded habit.

The closely allied honey locust, *Gleditsia triacanthos*, pro-duced one of the American patented trees with its selected form 'Sunburst'. Horizontally growing, more widely spaced branches and 'lighter' foliage give it a more feathery ap-pearance than 'Frisia'. The colour is that of the bright golden-yellow younger foliage against the rich, deep-green older leaves, a most exhilarating contrast all too seldom seen. But again there is a measure of brittleness in the branches—not uncommon in woody members of Leguminoseae—which ought to be capable of being countered by building up a more solid framework, although this would to some extent destroy the tiering of the branches which is a pleasing feature of a naturally grown tree.

When the golden magnificence of the hanging chains of flowers is spent the laburnums are rather unexciting as foliage trees. There is, however, something to be said for *Laburnum anagyroides (vulgare)* 'Aureum' with foliage which, to a degree, carries the bounteous period on through the summer months. This is its real hey-day for at flowering time there is little contrast for the flowers. It is well worthy of inclusion where there is a place for it although it has a tendency on occasion to attempt to return to the green of its parent.

Generally the Japanese maples are seen as large shrubs rather than the small bushy trees that most of them are capable of making given time, and also there is not much gold among them during the summer months. Perhaps this is just as well for the autumn is their show time; even then gold is liable to be outshone by the numerous cultivars which fade away in brilliant shades of crimson and scarlet. For the summer there is one really good cultivar in *Acer japonicum* 'Aureum' with very soft, yellow foliage with little inclination to go green as it ages. This one is fairly slow growing, even by comparison with the majority of its kin.

Golden Ground Coverers and Alpines

The golden-leaved form of the wood millet grass, *Milium effusum aureum*, so beloved by the late E. A. Bowles that it is now universally known as Bowles' golden grass, is a delight to behold in the dappled shade of trees and under such conditions it retains its colour better than in full sun. This grass will seed itself sparingly and breed true. Partial shade is also appreciated by *Lamium maculatum* 'Aureum', a perfectly good ground coverer if not quite so versatile as the type or its pink and white flowered forms.

On the other hand the golden marjoram, *Origanum vulgare* 'Aureum', likes sun and plenty of it combined with an open, well-drained soil, although one need by no means despair if neither factor quite measures up but be ready to accept an effect slightly inferior to a bright-golden carpet for the whole of the summer. But outward and visible form and colour is not the begin and end all in the plant world. Scent is appreciated by everyone, particularly those denied the precious gift of sight. In this respect aromatic foliage also has a part to play and the golden marjoram is one of many plants endowed with it, which we will consider in more detail later.

The golden meadow foxtail grass, *Alopecurus pratensis* 'Aureus', also likes the sun. Growing a foot or so high it is a most desirable ornamental grass, strictly speaking variegated for its leaves are banded with yellow but so broadly that, for the early part of the season at least, the bright colour quite

Hosta fortunei 'Aurea': delicate golden young foliage deepening to yellowish-green.

outshines the green.

The unfolding leaves of *Hosta fortunei* 'Albopicta' are bright yellow, edged green, and are a conspicuous feature until they gradually fade to a yellowish green around mid-summer. *H. fortunei* '*Aurea*' has similar attractions except that the leaves are initially wholly yellow. Even when this aura has passed they remain excellent, distinctive foliage plants and there is the pleasure of their pale lavender blooms to follow.

As a flowering plant *Filipendula ulmaria* 'Aurea' cannot compete with its parent the meadow sweet but has equal value for brightening up the waterside with its splash of gold, particularly in the spring when it is at its brightest and best, and there is grace and form in its finely divided leaves. Really moist soil or bog conditions are requisites and partial shade is not objected to.

Getting down more to ground level we have a tiny carpeter, *Sagina glabra* 'Aurea', a golden counterpart of the notorious pearlwort, that persistent weed of lawns and rock gardens and occupier, like the ubiquitous annual meadow grass, of any space in ground, gravel path or crevice in paving if it gets half a chance. Some question the wisdom of introducing its golden form into a garden but I doubt if it would ever become widespread and obnoxious for it does tend to die out in the winter and needs frequent replanting if it is not to fade away gradually. At least that is my experience in using it for permanent planting as opposed to carpet bedding, for which purpose it is admirably suited.

Then we have the golden form of the old creeping Jenny, *Lysimachia nummularia* 'Aurea', by no means as invasive as its parent. Like the *Sagina* it does not go through the winter without becoming a little dowdy but it is a useful golden carpeter for the less formal parts during the summer months.

Despite often unfounded fears of invasion no one would advocate either of the foregoing for the rock garden proper. Here one can be well served by the golden thyme, *Thymus vulgaris* 'Aureus', whose prostrate golden mats are just as aromatic when disturbed as those of the common thyme of moorlands and cliffs. To some the lemon-scented thyme may have more nostalgic attraction, in which case there is *T.* x *citriodorus* 'Aureus' to satisfy both senses.

While silver may be a more common variant among the saxifrages a spot of gold can always be introduced with *Saxifraga moschata* 'Cloth of Gold', valuable for the shady parts rather than full sunshine which perhaps the majority of golden-leaved plants relish. *Veronica teucrium* 'Trehane' is one of the most gleaming rock plants but unfortunately its foliage colour disappears for the winter as the plant is herbaceous. For a crevice in paving or some suitable gritty pocket in the rock garden one can with advantage employ the dwarf, golden mats of *Scleranthus biflorus*.

Now, having looked at some of the best and most attainable gold reserves we turn to silver which, from the garden point of view, is even more valuable for there is no competition from the floral side.

Silver in a garden, like gold, does need to be used with some reserve, but it is invaluable, not only to create patches or drifts of acceptable colour but to tone down, or act as a foil for, colours like magenta which tend to become harsh or blatant. Conversely, it will liven up dull purples and crimsons or form subtle pastel combinations with light mauves and pinks. Consequently there is always a place for it in a garden and, like gold, at no time is it more appreciated than during the winter months.

Trees and Shrubs

Apart from variegated foliage there are comparatively few trees of truly silver-grey appearance. Perhaps this is not a bad thing for if the choice was wide there could easily be over-planting—as with gold, great daubs of silver would tend to impart a feeling of artificiality to the landscape.

Pyrus salicifolia 'Pendula': an elegant small weeping tree with silvery-grey foliage.

The outstanding tree, other than the conifers, and one that is not likely to be anything but an asset to the scene when properly placed is the weeping willow-leaved pear, *Pyrus salicifolia* 'Pendula', which, when grown in standard form, makes a most elegant small tree with slender branches sweeping to the ground and clothed with narrow, silver-grey leaves.

There are several willows with silver-grey foliage but generally these are subjects for the waterside in the broader landscape. *Salix alba* 'Sericea' is, however, quite moderate in growth, making a round-headed tree of medium size only with most attractive foliage.

It is a pity that, even in small gardens, more use is not made of some of the dwarf, shrub-like willows. There is, for instance, the creeping willow, *S. repens*, which as its name implies is a prostrate shrub and one which makes excellent ground cover. Its variety *argentea* has silver-grey foliage and yellow catkins. Or one can turn to the woolly willow, *S. lanata*, perhaps even more silver in tone, not so much of a ground hugger but making a most attractive small, flat, somewhat-spreading shrub seldom more than 3ft high. *S. repens argentea* can be used with advantage as a weeping standard for planting in places where the willow-leaved pear would be out of proportion.

Senecio laxifolius (*S. greyi* of gardens) is a subject beloved by landscape architects as a leading silver-grey shrub in the 2-3ft high range with good, ground-covering capacity. Although it occasionally takes a hammering in a particularly severe winter it will usually break away again freely from lower down. It benefits from an annual cutting back in spring of the longest of the straggling growths to keep it compact and to prevent it becoming woodily gaunt in the centre.

The inability of *Convolvulus cneorum* to stand up to a really severe snap with penetrating east winds is much to be regretted. An occasional, but brief, low drop in temperature may do no more than 'scorch' but prolonged spells too often are fatal.

A dwarf, very shrubby species growing little more than a foot high, neat and tidy and with silvery hairs which give more shine than a tomentose covering, its beauty is enhanced by its white, typically convolvulus, flowers from pink buds opening in early summer.

Santolina is another popular dwarf shrub which can be grown with impunity in the southern counties even if not always quite happy further north. Treating as a sub-shrub by cutting hard back each spring removes winter aftermath, very much discourages flowering which really is no great asset to the intensely silver foliage, and keeps the whole plant from lapsing into a sprawling mass. S. chamaecyparissus (S. incana) is the most popular species, the dwarf form 'Nana' growing no more than 9-12in high being also very desirable. S. neapolitana is taller and has more finely divided leaves.

Artemisia, Helichrysum and Senecio

The great Compositae family has been most generous in providing plants with silver to grey foliage, as it has been to horticulture generally. None are more intensely silver than the numerous species and cultivars of Artemisia, Helichrysum and Senecio but with these, as with a number of plants with foliage of this colour, hardiness so often is dependent on having a well-drained soil and a sunny aspect, with no stagnation of moisture around the leaves and crowns during the winter. Silver in foliage is often provided, not by inner pigmentation but, by a covering of silvery hairs of varying lengths and densities on the leaves and stems, sometimes so congested that they form a woolly down. Here, of course, lies one of the reasons why, in many instances, there is a degree of susceptibility to surface and atmospheric moisture.

Among artemisias and helichrysums one takes one's choice for there are a dozen or more species and cultivars of varying habits and degrees of hardiness, all with delightfully intense silver foliage. One's choice will depend on the purpose to be

served and the associations desired and be finally governed by
the ability of the individual to prosper and survive in the
conditions which prevail. I shall, therefore, mention only a
few of the toughest and leave it to readers to delve further if
their conditions approach the ideal. One can always, of course,
play safe and raise a few replacements each year and this
generally presents few problems for most root easily from
cuttings assisted by a frame from which frost can be excluded.
In any event fresh stock occasionally is desirable as the old
plants often tend to get a little ragged after a year or so.

The common wormwood, *Artemisia absinthium*, so often
found well established around rubbish tips and derelict sites
vacated by human habitation, has through the late and lamented
Margery Fish given us an excellent cultivar in 'Lambrook

Artemisia ludoviciana 'Silver Queen': one of the best of the intensely silver
artemisias.

Silver'. Or in the 3ft high range we can consider *A. palmeri* from California or the white sage, *A. ludoviciana*, which adorns itself with plumes of tiny, silvery flowers in mid-summer. 'Silver Queen' with more finely divided leaves is a desirable form of this. *A. baumgartenii* (*A. villarsii*) is lower growing and more bushy with smaller much divided leaves. For even dwarfer and more compact habit there are *A. nutans* and *A. armeniaea* (*A. canescens*)—which by some are classed as variants of the sea wormwood, *A. maritima*—also *A. schmidtiana*, all with the finest filigree silvery foliage. To clothe the ground more completely or drape a dry rock face or wall one can profitably employ the foot high *A. stellerana*.

With *Helichrysum* it may also be a matter of latitude, site and soil. Probably one will find the silvery mats of *H. orientale* most likely to prosper, or it could be the taller *H. angustifolium*. One might achieve success with *H. fontanesii* or the ground covering *H. bellidioides*—all are silvery gems where the conditions are to their liking. *H. milfordiae* (*H. marginatum* of gardens) is one of my favourites. It forms a low mat of silver foliage with almost stemless, dainty, white flowers, pink tipped in bud and at the points of the involucre of petal-like bracts when fully open.

Senecio cineraria, which seems to get all tied up with *S. maritima* and *Cineraria maritima* as alternative names, has given us several useful silver-foliage cultivars. 'White Diamond', as intense silvery white as its name implies, has proved tolerably hardy and there seems no reason why similar success should not be possible with the newer 'Silver Dust' which is dwarfer and has more finely divided leaves. Again, as with artemisias and helichrysums there is safety in having a few young plants available to replace winter casualties.

More Silver Plants

Still with Compositae we turn to the milfoils; *Achillea ageratifolia* and *A. clavenae* are both silvery foliage plants with white flowers for the rock garden where a place should also be found for *Anthemis rudolphiana*, a neat growing plant producing a succession of deep-golden flowers from mid-summer onwards. Here, too, if space permits the sprawling mats of *A. cupaniana* can be profitably used to drape a rock face and provide white flower throughout the summer.

There is not really a lot to choose between *Anaphalis yedoensis* (perhaps to be known as *A. cinnomomea*), *A. margaritacea*, *A. triplinervis* and *A. nubigena*, except in height, *A. yedoensis* being about 2ft, *A. nubigena* a foot or so and the others around the 18in mark. All are good herbaceous plants with silvery-grey foliage and white 'everlasting' flowers extremely useful for drying. Also for the herbaceous border there is that old fashioned plant, *Lychnis flos-jovis*, sometimes referred to as the 'flower of love'. Silky hairs give a really silvery sheen to the foliage and there is quite a long spell of rosy-pink flowers from the end of June until August.

Euryops acraeus (*E. evansii* of gardens) is another desirable foliage plant, often grown under glass but pretty well hardy if given a hot, dry and sunny position outside. Neat and compact, a mere 12in high, its yellow flowers are in evidence for most of the summer and it is ideal for the front of the herbaceous border or for the rock garden where, given good companions, it will always be a pleasing sight.

Not many native plants, which are still fairly abundant in the wild, become occupants of our gardens. The horned poppy, *Glaucium flavum*, is a coastal plant and thus at home in sand and sun, but the richer moister soil of a garden does not materially affect its way of life and it may even be all the better for more generous treatment. Easily raised from seeds, which is just as well for it is not a very good perennial, the radical leaves are generously silvered, the large yellow, poppy-like flowers are a conspicuous feature for most of the summer months and are followed by long, curved, pod-like fruits up to 12in long.

One generally does not enthuse over plantains and while *Plantago argentea* may not be much lauded and sought after it is quite a useful silver-leaved plant and a 'white sheep' in a pretty weedy genus.

The low creeping mats of *Raoulia australis* always fascinate me. Growing a mere inch or so high it can be used to underplant some of the more shrubby alpines, but being a native of New Zealand, it does need full exposure to the sun and a light, very well drained soil.

Sedums there are in plenty, several with glaucous leaves and none more silvery in tone with white farina during the summer than *S. spathulifolium* 'Purpureum' whose leaves, as they begin to age, live up to the varietal name by turning to a mealy deep purple to help warm up the colder months of the year. What attraction this plant has for blackbirds I shall probably never know, but from time to time they do have the urge to pull it apart and, indeed, propagate it for many of the pieces root on the surface of the soil. *S. spathulifolium* 'Capa Blanca' retains its silvery coating throughout without any change of hue.

There are numerous silver saxifrages for a sunny position on the rock garden, from the tiny cultivars of *Saxifraga aizoon* to the 2ft arching plumes of *S.* 'Tumbling Waters', their neat rosettes of encrusted leaves being a joy in or out of flower.

Known best as a component of carpet bedding schemes, *Antennaria dioica* can do equally valuable service as a close silver carpeter in rock garden or paving, even in a gravel path or the front of a shrub border as a protective blanket and foil for the smaller bulbs. It provides an all-the-year-round effect although the older leaves do go a little grey green in winter. When it produces its white or pink flowers on 6-9in stems one gets the urge to remove them hastily for in themselves they have no great virtue and rather detract from the foliage. They do, however, make quite valuable material if cut at the right stage for drying for winter floral arrangements.

Say what you will about its territorial ambitions there is no more attractive or efficient silver ground cover than the old snow-in-summer, *Cerastium tomentosum*. Never despise it where its foliage and sheet of white flowers can be used with advantage to cover an unsightly bank or derelict spot and repel most other invaders but always make sure its aspirations are kept very much in check for it is an underground rather than a surface rooter and considerably more difficult to eradicate once it gets a foothold.

The large woolly leaves of the lamb's ear, *Stachys olympica* (*S. lanata*), would appear to invite trouble from winter damp and foraging slugs but this is in fact quite a reliable winterer in all but the wettest of soils. Retaining at least the youngest leaves throughout the winter it can be termed evergreen and is one of the finest of the more vigorous silver carpeting plants for sun and, indeed a certain amount of shade. Flowering does not add to its attractions for the stems are casual rather than constant in production, looking as if they have just strayed in and with nothing compelling about their flowers. It is just as well to remove them when they appear or, better still, grow only the non-flowering form known as 'Silver Carpet'.

Large silvery, woolly leaves are also the main talking point with *Verbascum bombyciferum* (*V. broussa*), rather than the yellow flowers clothing the giant 6-8ft stems. These are, however, quite acceptable and, together with the outstanding foliage, have much architectural value during the summer. Although the plant is a biennial it seeds itself quite freely and the seedlings while on their way towards providing for the following summer are very effective with their foliage in this in-between season. *Salvia argentea* is also classed as a biennial with a more prolonged existence if it is not allowed to flower— and this is no great loss. When I first employed this plant for its foliage I had no great hopes of the large, woolly leaves surviving a wet winter but this they did and also one of some severity.

Onopordon acanthium: a silvery 'thistle' of great character.

The Scotch thistle, *Onopordon acanthium*, is a great imposing thistle-like plant of biennial character which seeds itself quite freely. Towering to a height of 6ft when it pushes up its branched stems surmounted with rosy-purple flowers it needs fairly spacious surrounds and companions in proportion. In the right setting its large, silver-grey, woolly leaves and statuesque habit make it a most impressive sight.

Those words 'impressive sight' constitute a reminder that both gold and silver in a garden can become the cynosure of all eyes and that the acme of perfection in their use can only be achieved if, like money, they are used wisely and often sparingly. Lashed about they can reduce the more homely things to insignificance or considerably disturb harmony, and harmony of all things is priceless to those who really appreciate the finer points of a garden.

CHAPTER FOUR

From Silver to Grey

WITH FOLIAGE, perhaps even more so than with flowers, it is often difficult to determine the line of demarcation between hues. Where does silver end and grey begin, when is green reached and where do we link up with bluish-greens, glaucous sheens and the metallic tints? Perhaps, therefore, there is reason for excuse if a few of my subjects appear to be dealt with somewhat out of place.

Groping where to begin I cannot offend anyone if I give lavender pride of place and leave it at that for it needs no further description. Old world charm and sentimentality can be further satisfied with the grey, feathery, aromatic leaves of *Artemisia abrotanum*, commonly called southernwood, lad's love or old man according to one's choice and past memories. Closely linked is rosemary for remembrance, *Rosmarinus officinalis*, which in addition to its grey, aromatic foliage is a blue-flowered shrub of appreciable charm, not forgetting there are several forms such as 'Benenden Blue' with brighter blue flowers and 'Miss Jessop's Upright' which makes a fine ornamental hedge.

Tougher than most in the genus are two dwarf-spreading hebes, *H. pinguifolia* 'Pagei' (*H. pageana*) and *H. pimeloides* 'Glaucocoerulea', valuable alike as evergreen ground coverers with glaucous-blue foliage and white and lavender flowers respectively. Also deservedly popular is *Caryopteris* which is planted mainly for the late summer blue of the flowers but whose grey-green appearance is more than useful for blending in with other flower and foliage hues. The blue spiraea, *C.* x *clandonensis*, seems now to have taken over from one of its parents, *C. incanus* (*C. mastacanthus*), in the popularity lists and is a first class subject to use for toning in a shrub border. It should be pretty severely pruned each spring to keep it compact and free flowering.

The Russian sage, *Perovskia atriplicifolia*, could be more often employed to give variety to the shrub border, its upright form, grey-green foliage and long spikes of lavender-blue flowers—particularly fine in the form 'Blue Spire'—having earned for it the Award of Garden Merit way back in the thirties. Then in winter it still has character in the upright grey stems.

While the common sage, *Salvia officinalis*, is not to be despised for ornamental purposes its most widespread use is for culinary purposes. The rue, *Ruta graveolens*, is a herb of bygone days but the introduction of the form 'Jackman's Blue' has brought it back into prominence as an ornamental shrub. For blue-grey, steely foliage this subject is quite unsurpassed and it can be used with great effect to produce some charming foliage combinations. Pruning back hard each spring will keep it in compact form, 2ft or a little more in height.

In contrast *Cytisus battandierii* is a much larger and perhaps more showy shrub of somewhat heavy appearance with its strong growth and silky, silver-grey trifoliate leaves, each leaflet up to 3in long and half as wide. When the upright, cone-shaped inflorescences of deliciously scented golden-yellow flowers appear in June this is indeed a shrub of much distinction be it grown against a wall or out in the open where it is perfectly hardy. Unlike others of its race it will not refuse to break again if cut back into hard wood if it overgrows its position, although it is best to avoid this if possible by occasionally cutting out some of the strongest branches after flowering right down to their base, from which strong, young, replenishing shoots will soon arise. I once overpropagated this shrub and decided to use the surplus as an ornamental hedge, a decision I never regretted for it soon grew into a classy, grey-green barrier with a red brick background and became a source of much admiration.

Abutilon vitifolium makes a tall, fairly open shrub or even a small tree where it thrives in the open without wall protection for, unfortunately, it is not quite as hardy as one would wish. The three- or five-lobed leaves and the young stems are coated with greyish down and with the open habit create an elegance in growth and foliage which is not present in all shrubs. The flowers, 2-3in across when open, violet-blue in the type and white in *alba*, make this also a most desirable flowering shrub, where it will succeed.

Among the shrubby potentillas there are several which add grey-green foliage to flowers freely produced over a long season, none more so than cultivars of *Potentilla fruticosa* like the yellow flowered 'Vilmoriniana', the low growing 'Beesii' and 'Mandschurica' with yellow and white flowers respectively and the spreading white flowered 'Abbotswood'.

The seaside gardener is almost sure to make use of the salt resistant sea buckthorn, *Hippophae rhamnoides*, and the tree purslane, *Atriplex halimus*, the first rather grey-green and the *Atriplex* of more silvery metallic sheen. Further inland they can also be used for foliage effect, plus the bonus of the brilliant scarlet berries of *Hippophae* provided there is the right admixture of the sexes to ensure pollination for the genus is dioecious. Both *Hippophae* and *Atriplex* are rather rampant and therefore not really suitable for the small garden.

Also a typical coastal shrub, the Jerusalem sage, *Phlomis fruticosa*, adds wrinkled leaves, grey-green on the upper surface and hairily white beneath, to its terminal whorls of yellow flowers. It succeeds also further inland in a light soil although in the colder districts it may be severely cut back in a hard winter.

Senecio monroi tends to be overshadowed by *S. laxifolius*, probably because its foliage is a quieter shade of grey-green, although covered with whitish felt beneath and attractively wrinkled. Generally I have found it a little more liable to frost damage than *laxifolius* and is, therefore, better suited to the warmer coastal regions where it will make a quite dense compact shrub some 3ft high and flower freely in July. Likewise there are some doubts as to the complete hardiness of *Hoheria* (*Plagianthus*) *lyallii* but this is always worth a gamble given reasonable conditions for it is a decided acquisition as a large shrub or small tree with grey, downy leaves and white, mallow-like flowers in mid summer.

Several of the shrub roses have tasteful grey-green foliage to add to the beauty of their flowers and provide foliar contrast to compensate for any intermittent flowering. *Rosa alba* 'Celeste' is one of the choicest for its combination of grey-green with soft pink flowers. Or one can opt for 'Maiden's Blush' or choose 'Stanwell Perpetual' because it is more continuous flowering. For the front of the border there is the neat little *R. chinensis* hybrid called 'Hermosa', with *R. brunonii* filling a need when an attractive foliage rose is required to cover a wall or scramble up an old tree.

Where there is plenty of space, and especially where shelter from coastal winds needs to be provided, *Elaeagnus* 'Ebbingei' will do the job admirably. It may not appeal to all but I find its evergreen leaves, thinly scaly above and more definitely silvered beneath, singularly attractive.

Other trees and shrubs not previously mentioned have foliage which is silvery beneath. The silver lime, *Tilia tomentosa* (*T. argentea*), takes its name from the white tomentose undersurface of the leaves, so delightful when viewed from beneath or at a distance when the foliage is rippling in

the breeze. *Sorbus aria* 'Lutescens' with its silvery upper surface gradually changing to grey-green as the summer advances
prolongs the charm of its unfurling foliage and that of the
type. Silvery undersurfaces are to be found in several species
of *Elaeagnus*, in *Berberis verruculosa*, *B. candidula* and other
barberries, and while their full value tends to be somewhat
hidden away it does add to their general attractions.

Grey-foliaged Heathers

The indispensable heathers are no longer grown primarily
for their long lasting floral display. Most of the garden cultivars
of the crossed-leaved heath, *Erica tetralix*, have distinctly grey-
green foliage, none more outstanding in this respect than
'Alba Mollis' which, in a heath garden, is sure to be joined for
floral effect by such beautiful cultivars as 'Con Underwood',
'L.E. Underwood' and others. The ling, *Calluna vulgaris*,
gives us 'Hirsuta Typica' and 'Silver Queen', both with
woolly, silver-grey foliage and barely distinguishable from each
other in herbage or in their light mauve flowers. Indeed, by
some they are regarded as identical.

Herbaceous Plants and Ground Coverers

Hostas keep cropping up in this book and not without real
justification. Here we must call attention to one of the most
majestic, *H. sieboldiana elegans*, magnificent in form accentuated by the bluish-grey leaves, a plant of outstanding character
whether it be placed in the woodland, by the water's edge or
in any shady corner, with or without its very pale-lilac
flowers. Self-sown seedlings are produced in plenty and should
not be allowed to form a colony for although a great group of
this splendid subject would not come amiss I do feel its
character is best displayed when it stands alone as a single
clump some 2ft high with a spread of a yard or more. *H.
fortunei* 'Hyacinthina' has all the attributes of *sieboldiana*
'elegans' with rather more definitely lilac flowers.

One still thinks affectionately of the plume poppy as *Bocconia* rather than *Macleaya cordata* and feels that its 5-6ft stems carrying glaucous leaves and panicles of creamy-white flowers are far more effective with a natural background than when forced to masquerade as overlord at the back of an herbaceous border. Imposing plants such as this, especially when the foliage is as outstanding as the flowers, always look

Hostas: always impressive plants whether in natural surroundings or associated with buildings.

better in a natural setting unencumbered and hemmed about by a host of brightly coloured and at times sophisticated neighbours.

I will but mention here but will not dwell upon the grey-green leaves of the globe artichoke, *Cynara scolymus*, or the more glaucous hue of the cardoon, *C. cardunculus*, and the seakale, *Crambe maritima*, those once popular culinary plants whose aesthetic majesty warrants their inclusion later.

The steely-grey foliage and blue flower heads of *Eryngium* and *Echinops* add much to the appearance of the herbaceous border. So too does the grey-green of *Centaurea dealbata* whose cultivar 'John Coutts' is very much superior to the type. Here too, very good use can be made of the grey foliage and deep blue flowers of *Veronica incana*. *Achillea* 'Moonshine' is a most desirable herbaceous plant with pale-yellow, flat heads of flower and finely cut silvery-grey foliage. Together these make a plant of considerable charm and one which will form happy colour associations with other plants, especially those with blue or mauve flowers. It is also first class for cutting.

The magnificent tree poppy from California, *Romneya coulteri*, with great white flowers with protruding boss of golden stamens, is an aristocratic sub-shrub suitable for associating either with shrubs or herbaceous perennials. Spreading by underground stems, when planted in good, well-drained soil in a sunny position it firmly establishes itself to belie the suggestion that it is a plant essentially for the warmer parts of the country. Its glaucous-grey foliage at all times adds to the glamour of its spectacular flowers.

The catmints, *Nepeta* x *faassenii*, for long known as *N. mussinii*, and its more vigorous counterpart popularly called 'Six Hills Giant', somehow never look misplaced whether their situation be the herbaceous border, a rocky bank, crowning a dry wall or consigned to fringing the front of the shrub border. In all these situations they make excellent ground cover. Throughout the summer their grey-green aromatic mass and lavender-blue flowers is a stand-by—and most effective if not overdone—in countless gardens. As a contrast, and also for a shady situation, the grey-green leaves and white flowers of *Potentilla alba* have a great deal of merit.

The blood-root, *Sanguinaria canadensis*, is a ground coverer in a different vein for it has rather more territorial ambitions although it is not really disposed to make a nuisance of itself. This is a plant which grows in sun or shade but really prefers some relief from the midday sun. In conditions reasonably cool and moist it will spread steadily by means of thick horizontal root-stocks. The white flowers on 6in stems are quite chaste and, for once in a while, the double flowered form, 'Flore Pleno', is to me even more desirable. The flowers are, perhaps, not quite in keeping with the large, crenate, glaucous-grey leaves but appear before these are fully expanded and are in no danger of being engulfed. Throughout the summer this foliage makes a pretty effective weed barrier.

For the Rock Garden
The acaenas are carpeters rather than weed excluders and form a more than useful base coat for small bulbs on the rock garden as well as displaying restful foliage colour. Here the grey-green, metallic tones of *A. buchananii* are always welcome to help counter any reaction when the spring plethora of floral colour has faded. *A. adscendens* is similar but taller and a rather more effective barrier to weeds.

The thymes too contribute to the summer attractions of the rock garden with foliage as well as flowers, especially the grey, woolly aromatic mats of *T. pseudolanuginosus* and *T. hirsutus doerfleri*.

Hypericum polyphyllum and *H. olympicum* are really distinct but confused in gardens. The plant I grow as *polyphyllum*, quite apart from several weeks spell when the foliage is literally blotted out by the masses of quite large golden, fluffy-stamened flowers, is throughout the summer a welcome tidy, glaucous-green boss of foliage on the rock garden.

Among the helianthemums, so brilliant and welcome with their spell of floral beauty after the spring flush is tailing off, we should always include a few with grey-green foliage for its value during the rest of the year. I am particularly fond of 'Mrs Croft' with delicate pink, suffused orange flowers and foliage more silvery-grey than most. Then there is the startling orange-red 'Henfield Brilliant', the creamy-white 'The Bride', the crimson 'Supreme', the golden 'Praecox' and others with much foliage value.

Lobularia (*Alyssum*) *maritimum* is planted for its great hummocks of gold or lemon spring flowers but it is also a grey-green foliage plant of merit once the aftermath of the old flowering stems has been cleared. Too often it dominates a rockery in a small garden when it might be better placed as a frontal plant in a flower border or effectively and restfully covering up some odd corner, making perhaps fuller use of its foliage than its early blaze of floral colour.

Ornamental Grasses

These are not used to the extent they ought to be in gardens. The larger, more robust ones stand out as plants of some character, imparting diversity and form in habit, foliage and flowering stems. The dwarfer ones can be used for group or under planting and also, on occasion, as edgings to beds or borders of other subjects. There is no situation where a few cannot be used to good effect, be it the fringes of the woodland or shrub plantings, the herbaceous border, formal bedding and, in particular, in association with water. One of the neatest and most useful is the steely, blue-grey form of the sheeps fescue, *Festuca glauca*, which makes compact tufts of foliage some 9-12in high with flower spikes of similar coloration extending just above the foliage and never leaving an aftermath of seedlings to become a nuisance. Indeed, the plant as a whole just steadily grows a little larger and never transgresses.

Festuca glauca: a neat glaucous-grey grass useful for both informal and formal planting.

F. glacialis is a dwarfer 6in high counterpart while the taller *F. eskia* (*F. crinum-ursi*) is much more of a spreader, gradually extending by creeping rootstocks into an excellent ground covering mat.

These festucas do die down during the winter and are best left with their mat of dead grass intact until just before growth starts in spring when they can be trimmed over.

Two evergreen bluish-grey grasses are well worthy of inclusion in the landscape and garden. Where the view is broad and especially when the coastal gardener has patches of windswept sand to clothe and stabilise, there is no more effective subject than the lyme grass, *Elymus arenarius*. This is invasive and not at all suitable for the average-to-small garden but where there is space, sandy soil and a job that needs doing the creeping rootstock and 2ft high glaucous, blue-green foliage with 4-5ft flower spikes will prove invaluable. On the other hand, where invasive tendencies must be frowned upon the 18in steel blue-grey clumps and 3ft flower spikes of *Helictotrichon sempervirens* (*Avena sempervirens* or *A. candida*) will be most useful and effective.

Although we invariably plant for flowers alone we must not overlook the fact that some of our most popular garden kinds do also provide us with a deal of silvery-grey stability to mellow down the bright colours and to contrast with the greens. Few gardens are devoid of hardy pinks and carnations and bearded irises which have their season of floral glory, all too brief, and for the rest of the year have foliage which, if one will only stop to appreciate it, makes perhaps an even greater contribution to the overall picture.

CHAPTER FIVE

Variegated Foliage

By VIRTUE OF its generally irregular admixture of, in the main, silver or gold with the basic green, variegated foliage in too large or too many doses can become a little sickly, so again taste and good judgement must be the order in its employment. Treated with the deference it deserves, in the broad picture it will impart character as well as lightness and relief.

Perhaps it is the dogwoods which are most likely to be overdone for there are several variegated forms which are common denizens of the garden, partly because they are so adaptable. Any soil, particularly if it is wet or chalky, sun or partial shade, grimy industrial or salt sprayed coastal areas all come pretty much alike to *Cornus alba* and its cultivars, among which most of the good variegated forms are to be found. Adding to the foliage there are bright red stems for winter effect, none finer than 'Westonbirt' which, unfortunately, has quite ordinary green foliage. For golden variegation the undoubted favourite is 'Spaethii' but I have more than a sneaking liking for 'Gouchaltii' which is not quite so vigorous and which sometimes shows traces of pink in its yellow-margined leaves. 'Elegantissima' ('Sibirica Variegata') is a quite outstanding silver-variegated form.

The richly golden 'Maculata' ('Aureo-Variegata') form of *Elaeagnus pungens* always stands out among its neighbours. By and large I very much like or just as strongly dislike where golden variegation is concerned. Here is one of my favourites for the gold is concentrated into a large patch in the centre of each leaf and not haphazardly dispersed. This makes it literally glow, particularly in the winter and while it will ultimately make a very large, sparsely but strongly spiny, shrub it is not really fast growing and takes quite a few years to become too large for the average-sized garden; and its ultimate attainment may well be deferred by the attraction of an odd snippet in a floral arrangement.

I am also very partial to *Weigela* (*Diervilla*) *florida* 'Variegata' as a foliage variant in the shrub border or, again, as a provider of cut material when its somewhat arching branches carry a profusion of pale pink, tubular flowers which, perhaps rather unexpectedly, blend in beautifully with the pleasantly, not harshly, cream-variegated foliage.

Kerria japonica 'Picta' is by no means as vigorous as the popular spring-flowering type, neither is it quite as hardy, but where extra severe winters are not commonplace it is worth a place in any shrub border for it has a lot of elegance and its silver-variegated foliage is quite pleasing to the eye. When the golden flowers are produced they combine most effectively with the silvery tracery of the foliage.

Daphnes always strike a chord for early floral beauty and fragrance, with *D. mezereum* predominating and sometimes causing heartaches by suddenly deciding to die for no obvious reason. The genus is rich in gems and there is at least one, *D. odora* 'Aureo-marginata', well worthy of a trial for its cream-margined evergreen leaves, let alone the compelling fragrance of its pinkish-white flowers opening any time from February to April. This seems to be quite hardy, certainly more so than the type, in sun or shade—indeed, I have it growing in a position where no more than the minimum of dappled sunlight penetrates for a short period each day during the summer, and it happily competes with the thirsty, groping roots of silver birches.

Another silver-variegated evergreen shrub for shade, but this time requiring a lime-free soil, *Pieris japonica* 'Variegata' is slow growing and compact and as such is very useful for livening up the front of a planting of subjects requiring similar conditions. *Euonymus fortunei* (*radicans*) 'Silver Queen' is another first-class, slow-growing foliage shrub no more than 2ft high and extremely useful for frontal and ground cover purposes. Or one can get even closer to the earth with 'Variegatus', both positively, but tastefully, silver-variegated evergreens.

There are numerous forms of *E. japonicus* whose evergreen leaves are marked or margined with silver or gold. Although those who garden selectively in the more salubrious areas may turn aside from them, where not so congenial town conditions or the wind and salt spray of the coast have to be combated *E. japonicus* and its forms can usually be relied on in sun or shade, and used for background planting or given more conspicuous quarters, and for hedge making.

Equally as accommodating and often maligned because it consents to flourish in the face of most plant hardships, the old spotted laurel, *Aucuba japonica*, still cannot be ignored even if no limitations of locality are imposed. One can, of course, get away somewhat from the commonplace by choosing the more elite forms such as 'Crotonoides'. Always with the spotted laurel it is worth ensuring there is the odd, less interesting, male plant around to do the necessary for a crop of large, red berries ripening in late winter on the variegated female plants.

Hollies variegated in gold and silver need no further introduction. Among the numerous cultivars with such foliage one can single out *Ilex* 'Golden King'—this like its counterpart 'Silver Queen' is a misnomer for the sexes do not tally with the names—which has broad leaves margined with gold, sparsely spined, on a compact bush. Often mistaken for a holly but far less frequently planted and deserving of a place in the shrub border or elsewhere because they are not rapidly space demanding, are the silver and gold margined cultivars of *Osmanthus heterophyllus* called respectively 'Variegatus' and 'Aureo-marginatus'.

Were it not for a tendency to 'burn' at the tips during the winter one could recommend *Viburnum tinus* 'Variegatus' without reserve. Instead one has to say that for the more balmy areas this is a shrub whose golden variegation can be enjoyed to the full at all seasons but particularly during the winter when it reaches its highest value. Much the same goes for *Hebe* x *franciscana* 'Variegata' if away from the coast where it thrives and seems completely immune to gales and salt spray and its broadly margined with gold leaves can provide colour among the greens, especially when joined by the blue flowers.

Griselinia littoralis and its white variegated form are, as the specific name infers, essentially shrubs for coastal areas, yet I have found the type quite easy and hardy in the industrial north. This makes one feel that both should be more universally planted for as foliage shrubs they have much to commend them. The variegated forms of *Buxus* are not usually rated high class but perform a more than useful role in alleviating basic and background planting in any soil, in sun or in shade.

After an initial lack of appreciation I have since grown rather more disposed towards the silver variegated cultivar of *Buddleia davidii*, appropriately called 'Harlequin', particularly when its foliage is surmounted by the reddish-purple flowers in late summer. A watch must, however, be kept for shoots with all green leaves which, if not removed, can speedily make a take-over bid.

Hydrangea macrophylla 'Variegata' is a shrub of considerable quality. So too is *Coronilla glauca* 'Variegata' but this one is not completely hardy and does require the protection of a warm wall. While the steely-blue foliage of *Ruta graveolens* 'Jack-mans' Blue' may serve a more specific purpose for foliage effect a place should also be found for 'Variegata', a shrub also of quite moderate proportions and with foliage variegated and bordered with creamy-white, the points of many of the young shoots being almost completely yellowish-cream until the leaves begin to fully open and mature.

Variegated Trees

There are comparatively few good variegated trees and of these *Acer platanoides* 'Drummondii' is a particular favourite of mine. By no means as fast growing as the Norway maple itself, its leaves are broadly margined with creamy-white, a much more definite and pleasing combination than the variegated syca-more, *A. pseudoplatanus* 'Leopoldii' where the mature leaves are splashed with yellowish-pink and purple and tend to strike a discordant note, especially at close quarters. I think this is often so with streaky or dappled variegation, although the overall effect at a distance may be quite harmonious. *A. pseudoplatanus* 'Nizettii', where a pinkish hue creeps in with the white, strikes a similar chord but, again, this is a tree to view at a distance rather than at very close quarters.

The Japanese angelica tree, *Aralia elata*, often grown as *A. chinensis* and also as *Dimorphanthus mandschuricus*, commands attention for its imposing foliage alone, even more so when its cultivars 'Aureo-variegata' and 'Variegata' add pleasing varie-gated colour. Allowed to grow into large shrubs or sparsely branched trees or, inhumanly but most effectively, cut hard back periodically to produce long strong growths clad with really massive leaves, the species and its foliage variants will stand out anywhere.

The variegated box elders, *A. negundo* 'Elegans' ('Elegant-issima') and 'Variegatum', with golden and silver variegation respectively, are agreeable if not too liberally employed. So too is *Fraxinus pensylvanica* 'Variegata' where the creamy-white is both marginal and mottled.

Young trees of *Populus* 'Aurora' will instantly attract attention. I have not, as yet, seen a fully grown tree but, like most poplars, it is a very strong grower in the early years and should be capable of attaining major proportions. Its leaves are quite large and when young are broadly banded with creamy white round the margins. Against the older, almost completely green, leaves this makes the tree quite distinct and pleasing and as growth continues well into the summer it is not just an

Aralia elata 'Aureo-variegata': large striking foliage of tropical appearance.

early passing phase. With maturity the creamy white becomes absorbed in the green and towards late summer when growth tails off the overall effect tends to wane. I am told that this tree is now being used quite successfully as a shrub for banks etc, being stooled down annually resulting in extra vigorous growth and leaves more liberally banded with cream than when grown naturally.

The Cornelian cherry, *Cornus mas*, is usually grown as a large bush but it does make a neat, small, round-headed tree when taken up on a leg. 'Variegata', with leaves margined with white can be grown in similar form to provide quietly attractive foliage following the late winter burst of yellow blossom on the leafless branches. *C. controversa* 'Variegata' is even more compelling as a bushy, foliage tree. By comparison with the fairly large, oval, green leaves of the type its foliage is much smaller, being rather irregularly lanceolate with a certain deformed, but not tortured, look about it. The glossy green is confined to the centre of each leaf blade and is surrounded by a fairly broad irregular band of creamy white. This is altogether a fascinating, interesting and rather uncommon tree deserving of wider recognition.

Likely to become quite popular when more readily obtainable, the variegated tulip tree, *Liriodendron tulipifera* 'Aureomarginatum' has the typical and unusual square-cut leaves of the type broadly edged with yellow which deepens to yellowish green as they age. Major trees of upstanding form which, through their bright or yellowish-green foliage, stand out at a distance are always of value in the broader landscape and one can be sure that both the tulip tree itself and its variegated cultivar will make a worth-while contribution throughout the summer and especially at leaf fall.

Valuable Climbers

Among climbing plants perhaps the most striking of all is *Actinidia kolomikta* whose fairly large, ovate-cordate leaves

Actinidia kolomitka: many of the leaves almost wholly creamy-white flushed with pink.

start the season in the traditional green. Then white variegation begins to creep in until as much as the whole, but more
often a good half, of the leaf surface becomes pinkish-white.
The leaf coloration is brought out best when planted against
a sunny wall.

All too seldom seen is the yellowish-white variegated form
of the summer jasmine, *Jasminum officinale* 'Aureo-variegatum',
a most effective plant for a wall and, being a semi-evergreen
like the type, it does retain its foliage well into the winter.
But among variegated climbing plants there are none more
accommodating and useful than the ivies, be they utilised as
climbers or merely assigned the role of covering the ground.

Generally one sees the large-leaved kinds, either *Hedera
colchica* 'Dentata Variegata' or *H. canariensis* 'Variegata'
('Gloire de Marengo') and these can be most colourful,
especially when they approach the limit of their support and
the growths branch out into bushy form, the leaves become
almost entire and flowering and fruiting commences. Cuttings
from these growths will, as is well known, produce bushy,
non-climbing plants and I think it is a great pity that this
strange freak of nature is not more fully exploited. They do
make excellent bushes which are invaluable for planting under
trees where so many shrubs are not at all happy. Both the
foregoing variegated forms are just as attractive when grown
in bush form, particularly *canariensis* 'Variegata' whose leaves
become charmingly streaked with crimson and purple during
the winter.

It is now more fully realised that most of the small-leaved
ivies so popular as house plants are perfectly hardy outside and
are even better than the large-leaved species for ground cover
where small areas have to be clothed. I started using these
several years ago for this purpose, finding the silver-variegated
Hedera helix 'Glacier' ideal and really quite a feature when
having reached a large old London plane it commenced its
upward passage. I had the happy thought of planting masses of

Hedera colchica 'Dentata Aurea': showing the almost entire creamy-yellow variegated leaves on the bushy flowering growths.

large purple and white crocuses in this carpet to create a delightful picture in the spring sunshine dappled with the shadows of the branches of the trees above. 'Chicago' and 'Goldheart' ('Jubilee') are also suitable for outside culture as are most of the green-foliaged cultivars.

I once came across a large modern housing estate where the dividing walls were being clad literally with masses of *Lonicera japonica* 'Aureo-reticulata'. This is a pretty climber with small leaves daintily reticulated and mottled in accordance with its name but not one to be used and repeated in great doses which impart nausea. Had the masses been broken up here and there, as on my own garage wall, with the odd purple *Clematis* 'Gipsy Queen' or other contrasting colour some quite delightful combinations could have resulted.

Variegated Grasses

The grass family is not as well represented in gardens as it ought to be, apart from the ever popular lawn. Perhaps the most use is made of the old gardener's garters, *Phalaris arundinacea* 'Picta' whose tall clumps of white striped leaves spread quite freely and can slowly become invasive. Equally as effective as a tall foliage plant and more content to stay at home, *Miscanthus sinensis* (*Eulalia japonica*) provides the forms 'Variegatus' with white striped leaves and 'Zebrinus' which is attractively cross banded with yellow. I like to see all these tall grasses used to give broad effect, even in partial shade, rather than as an addition to the formal border, especially when they are backed by dark or purple-foliaged trees or shrubs.

Dwarfer, around the 2ft high mark, *Molinia coerulea* 'Variegata' can be used as a weed suppressor in places where it can wander without causing concern. The variegated Yorkshire fog, *Holcus mollis* 'Variegatus' is quite dwarf but can also be invasive. *Dactylis glomerata* 'Variegata' too is dwarf but more clump forming and does appreciate periodic lifting, dividing and replanting when used permanently outside.

For the waterside *Glyceria maxima* 'Variegata' is a handsome grass of major proportions with variegations in creamy-yellow and white. The false oat grass, *Arrhenatherum elatius* 'Bulbosum Variegatum', is a useful variegated form suitable for a situation where its invasive tendencies will not become an embarrassment.

The sweet flag, *Acorus calamus*, together with *A. gramineus*, are also plants for the waterside and both have desirable variegated forms. Although aroids, and so far removed from the grasses, in their foliage they are grass-like, particularly *A. gramineus* which is the dwarfer of the two species. Much more closely related to the true grasses, the common wood rush, *Luzula maxima*, is a rampant, invasive subject but extremely valuable as a ground coverer and weed suppressor in the deep dry shade beneath trees or on difficult to maintain banks. The form 'Variegata' ('Marginata') has cream coloured

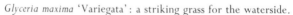

Glyceria maxima 'Variegata': a striking grass for the waterside.

margins to the leaves and is somewhat less rampant in habit.

Ground Cover and Woodland

The variegated yellow archangel *Galeobdolon luteum* 'Varie-gatum' (*Lamium galeobdolon* 'Variegata') is another rampager with similar ability to clothe a difficult spot. Capable of making 3ft or more of growth a year it is in its glory and at its most useful best when space is limitless. The silver mottling of its leaves, more pronounced in the winter, provides a charming blanket all the year round. Commonly offered at garden centres and often openly advocated for ground cover without due warning of its burning desire to spread out in all directions it too often finds its way into a quite small garden where it either becomes a nuisance or cannot do justice to itself.

On the other hand *L. maculatum* wanders in a more limited way by self-sown seedlings, is never a nuisance but a perfectly good ground coverer which is easy to control. The leaves, with a central silvery stripe are always appealing and provide a good foil to soften the rather harsh purplish-pink flowers and make a patch in the right setting—quite a floral feature in the early summer. Even more acceptable as flowering plants, still with ornamental foliage, are *roseum* with medium pink flowers and *album*.

The pleasantly aromatic round-leaved or apple mint, *Mentha rotundifolia*, goes one better with 'Variegata' which is a really silvery plant, often with shoots completely white. A good coloniser, but not to the point of being really invasive, this is a quite delightful foliage plant of medium height, happiest in moist soil and eminently suitable for the fringes of the waterside, where it makes a charming companion and ground cover for the dark-foliaged, scarlet flowered *Lobelia fulgens*.

The hostas always display character be they green or one of the desirable variegated forms, and always their flowers,

mainly in shades of soft mauve or lilac with the occasional
white, are a great asset in mid summer. They are without
doubt among the finest of shade-loving plants provided that
shade does not mean parched conditions at the roots for
moisture they do appreciate although not to the extent of
waterlogging. On the fringes of the woodland, adjacent to the
waterside and in the shade of tall buildings they are supreme.
They can even be used in an herbaceous border without
looking out of place although such a situation seldom really
does them justice. And if needs be they are not averse to full
sunshine but hot, dry situations should be avoided.

Among the best variegated forms are *Hosta sieboldii* (*H.
albomarginata*', *H. fortunei* 'Marginata Alba', *H.* 'Thomas
Hogg' and *H. crispula*, all with creamy-white edges to the
leaves, the last named distinct as the edges are attractively
waved. With *H. ventricosa* 'Variegata' the colour variation is

Hosta undulata: one of the dwarfer hostas with leaves with waved edges and
broad creamy-white central bands.

a creamy-yellow along the margins, with *H. v.* 'Aureomacu-lata' it is a yellowish central band, while *H. undulata* has a quite broad creamy centre with waved edges. *H. undulata univittata* is a more vigorous form of this with a silvery-creamy band down the centre of each leaf.

The lungworts turn to the production of outstanding foliage after their very early flowers have faded, so one gets the best of both worlds. Both *Pulmonaria officinalis*, and *P. picta* (*P. saccharata*) have pink flowers turning to blue, both colours being in evidence at the same time to give an unusual and not displeasing effect. *P. picta* is known as the Bethlehem sage because it often flowers around Christmas time but generally one should not count on any real flush of bloom until late February. The large basal leaves which succeed the flowering stems are heavily spotted with white and are perhaps rather larger and more effective than those of *P. officinalis*. For ground cover purposes all the pulmonarias, including the green-leaved forms, are excellent where there is shade from the hot sun and adequate moisture down below.

No one can deny the value of *Pachysandra terminalis* for a similar purpose in a shady situation and neither it or its silver variegated form are averse to somewhat dry conditions at the roots. One would wish they both were not quite so tardy in spreading out after planting, although once established the urge to spread and dominate increases and a dense carpet which will persist for years is formed.

Also somewhat slower to spread out and thicken up than the green-foliaged type, the variegated periwinkles, *Vinca minor* 'Variegata' and *V. m.* 'Aureo-variegata' are, neverthe-less, much quicker at establishing themselves than the pachysandras. On the other hand, *V. major* 'Variegata' ('Elegantissima') in creamy-white variegation is almost as quick as its parent to take over a piece of ground. When choosing between *major* and *minor* in any of their forms for ground cover due account must be taken of the fact that the former at 15-18in is much the taller of the two, does not form such a uniform mat and is the less desirable for small areas and for association with low growing shrubs.

Brunnera macrophylla, which used to be called *Anchusa myosotidiflora*, is always liked for its forget-me-not like flowers in the spring and is a quite excellent foliage plant for the summer in shady conditions where it will slowly extend with a few odd seedlings. Its most alluring form 'Variegata', with leaves broadly edged with cream is all too rare in gardens and should be planted whenever obtainable and there is a shady corner to clothe and liven.

The masterwort, *Astrantia major*, is also a good clump forming ground coverer for a semi-shaded spot and like *Brunnera* has a quite classy foliage variant in 'Sunningdale Variegated' whose leaves are very positively marked yellow and creamy-yellow. Unfortunately the colour does tend to fade a little as the summer advances.

Plants which put forth their leaves during the winter and go to rest when the growing season is upon us are few and far between. The occasional freak in a garden is always a talking point but *Arum italicum* and its forms go one better in being a considerable asset. The type commences to push up its marbled leaves in the autumn and these die down after the spring flowers are over. There is appreciable variation in the degree of marbling and the forms known in gardens as 'Pictum' (autumn-flowering) and 'Marmoratum' are the best ones to have. Throughout the winter the large arrow or spear-shaped leaves make a most unusual and impressive feature on the sunny fringes of the woodland or waterside where the soil never really dries out.

Then there are the hardy cyclamen. Many, like the popular indoor strains of *C. persicum*, are prettily marked with silver. For this virtue, let alone for its flowers which are equal to any, and for its general adaptability, none can excel the silver marbling of the leaves of *C. hederifolium* (*C. neapolitanum*).

These appear above ground after the usually plentiful show of flowers in late summer and early autumn and stay with us until the next summer is close at hand.

Dwarf Plants and Carpeters

Unlike the purple-leaved form, the dwarf mats of *Ajuga reptans* 'Variegata' are always better in partial shade and a pleasure to behold throughout the summer, particularly when sprinkled with spikes of clear blue flowers from May to July. *Glechoma hederacae* (*Nepeta glechoma*) is another useful ground coverer for shade. In nature it wanders over the floor of woodlands and is commonly known as ground ivy although it bears no resemblance or has any relationship to ivy proper. One would hardly think of introducing the ordinary green form to gardens but its variegated counterpart which is often grown as a trailing plant in pots could be made much more use of in the open. Its leaves are heavily impregnated with white and it spreads and trails with abandon, sometimes getting into places it should not, but there are other invasive subjects which are much more difficult to control.

The aromatic thymes are always good to have around. The lemon-scented thyme, *Thymus* x *citriodorus*, has a most pleasing form in 'Silver Queen' which is silver round the edges of the tiny clustered leaves which imparts a sheen to the whole of the 9-12in mounds of foliage. *Sedum kamtschaticum* 'Variegatum' is a low growing stonecrop with creamy-white margins to the leaves lightly touched with pink at the very edges. It is a pity that *S. sieboldii* 'Variegatum' is not completely hardy for the leaves in whorls of three, occasionally four, have yellow centres and the whole makes a delicately pretty little plant. It is mainly grown as a pot plant but, being readily propagated, can often be used outside in the summer with advantage to clothe bare patches on the rock garden or temporarily to fill a crevice in paving or dry wall.

Erysimum (*Cheiranthus*) *linifolium* 'Variegatum' is an unusual little wallflower suitable for the rock garden or the forefront of the herbaceous border. Its leaves are broadly edged with cream and it is quite liberal with its violet-purple flowers which contrast nicely with the foliage. *Arabis caucasica (albida)* 'Variegata', similarly edged with creamy yellow but with white flowers, is also a valuable foliage plant for the rock garden and is often used as a component of formal spring bedding schemes. *Phlox amoena* 'Variegata' is a pretty little plant for draping rocks or for overhanging dry stone walls. The small leaves are edged and flaked with cream, stained pink at the extreme edge when they are unfurling.

No one with any feeling for plants can hardly fail to be filled with admiration for the old London pride, *Saxifraga umbrosa*, which I am told should now be *S. x urbium*. This correction of name sounds rather appropriate for although the plant is to be seen in many gardens it is as an occupant of the weediest scrap of a urban garden that it is, perhaps, best known and loved. It will grow practically anywhere and distinguish itself as a low, close ground coverer for all seasons whether the situation be open or shady, moist or dry, under some influence from tree roots, whatever the soil, coastal situation or inland, country or town. And only the foam flower, *Tiarella cordifolia*, can really match its candy-floss effects when the flowers appear en masse. Its child, 'Aurea Punctata' ('Variegata Aurea') whose leaves are blotched and mottled with yellow may not appeal to every artistic eye at close quarters but a patch viewed some little distance away may be quite attractive. While the type may be happy in sun or shade its progeny colours best in full sun, especially if the soil is not too rich, and while it also makes good ground cover it is somewhat slower to spread.

Other Variegated Plants

One of the most outstanding of variegated hardy plants is *Phlox* 'Norah Leigh'. Its purplish-pink flowers have no great value but the foliage, strongly marked with creamy yellow can be an outstanding feature, particularly if it is given a background of dark foliage or, even better, is associated with the blue or purple flowers of *Echinops ritro*, *Eryngium*, herbaceous salvias and other hardy plants of similar colour. And it will not look out of place away from the plant border, carefully sited and harmonised with shrubs like the mauve and reddish-purple cultivars of *Buddleia davidii*, with *Caryopteris* x *clandonensis* and the like.

The apparent variegation of *Eryngium variifolium* is really the silvery-green of the prominent mid-rib and main veins which make a broad tracery through the dark green leaves. *E. dichotomum* and other species also have this characteristic but rather less pronounced. These sea hollies naturally do best in a sandy soil and full sun but they will still cooperate if soil

Phlox 'Norah Leigh': a fine variegated plant for the herbaceous border.

conditions fall somewhat short of ideal provided there is free drainage.

Sedum alboroseum 'Foliis Medio-variegatum' is an attractive tall stonecrop whose fleshy leaves are broadly banded with yellow down the centre leaving narrow, green margins. The golden sage, *Salvia officinalis* 'Icterina' is a good bushy plant suitable for the front of either the herbaceous or shrub border and has foliage liberally, but not too loudly, variegated with gold. So too is the golden balm, *Melissa officinalis* 'Aurea', although this may well be reserved for the herb or aromatic garden, of which more anon.

Then there are the variegated irises, *I. pallida* 'Variegata' and *japonica* 'Variegata' for sunny, well drained sites, the latter with some shelter, *kaempferi* 'Variegata' and *pseudacorus* 'Variegata' for quite boggy ground and the evergreen *foetidissima* 'Variegata' for moist ground in shade where it will be a conspicuous feature in the autumn when the bursting seed pods reveal the orange-coated seeds.

In the wild garden there is a lot to be said for a form of the figwort, *Scrophularia aquatica* 'Variegata' (*S. nodosa* 'Variegata') which is liberally edged and flaked with creamy white. Its value is enhanced when it has a background and associates to bring out its best. Its flowers are of little consequence but this does not detract from the merit of the plant when placed in its right environment. They might just as well be removed to give added concentration to the foliage.

Also essentially a plant for the wilder parts of the garden, and indeed one whose self-sown seedlings will establish themselves among the rougher herbage, the biennial thistle-like *Silybum marianum* is, nevertheless, quite an imposing plant with a great deal of character. It grows to a height of some 4ft and has large, lobed, spiny leaves broadly and most attractively banded with silver along the main veins. Its common names of holy, blessed or our lady's milk thistle indicate attachments with religious circles and the roots, leaves and artichoke-like flower heads have all been put to culinary use in the past. I have come across seedlings of *Silybum* in the most unexpected of places, even at the base of a hedgerow where cattle regularly congregated to enjoy the shade of nearby trees in hot weather.

In somewhat similar vein, where there is adequate room to accommodate some of its self-sown seedlings and not to have at least one annual session uprooting them from around and in neighbouring plants, the variegated honesty, *Lunaria annua variegata* will naturalise and be a most conspicuous feature. The leaves have cream flaking in from the edges, becoming more pronounced in the upper parts of the plant until those leaves in the still elongating terminal flowering heads may be almost wholly cream, against which the violet-mauve flowers are most admirably displayed. The seedlings invariably have the variegation of their parents provided no plants of the ordinary green form are in the locality. Then, of course, when the seeds are cast the central membranes of the seed pods remain attached to the head of the plant to provide the popular dried material for winter home decorating.

CHAPTER SIX

Hues of Maroon, Purple and Bronze

OF THESE THREE colour descriptions, so far as foliage is concerned, one can regard purple as rather a misnomer for so often it is applied to foliage which is, strictly speaking, maroon *eg* the purple plum and the purple hazel. Seldom in outdoor plants do we come across any with leaves quite as near true purple as, for instance, the hot-house *Gynura aurantiaca*, but 'Purpurea' and 'Atropurpurea' as names for cultivars are so widely employed that I feel I must sandwich the simple adjective itself between the two other shades which more truly describe the colours which prevail.

Anything of deep coloration in a garden, be it a shade of green, crimson or purple, foliage or flowers, will impart a certain amount of solid warmth. Just as discretion is necessary in the amount of golden, silver and variegated foliage to use so with these dark shades which are apt to impart an opposite sombre effect when used in depth. Certain floral colours will clash; others like white, cream, primrose and pale pink will help to lighten them up and bring them into relief—indeed, prominence—to form special colour features.

But I must not dwell on colour combinations for, to a degree, debated in depth they can become personal inclinations or even antipathies. Rather must I do justice to a number of trees, shrubs and plants which provide valuable, deeply-coloured foliage for the discerning eye to exploit to the best advantage.

Perhaps the most widely known and used tree is the purple plum, variously known as *Prunus cerasifera atropurpurea* and *P. cerasifera pissardii*, a tree which at times is rather over-planted. Used with moderation and judgement it, or one of its close allies, cannot be omitted from any garden other than the merest patch. *P. cerasifera* 'Nigra' is even deeper in foliage tone and has larger, ·deeper pink flowers against the pinkish-white of *atropurpurea*. *P. x blireana* is not quite so accommodating in an exposed position but given reasonable, not necessarily sheltered, siting makes a delightful, somewhat smaller tree with double pink blossoms and foliage not quite so deeply coloured as the foregoing.

Rather more use could be made of the purple-leaved black-thorn, *P. spinosa* 'Purpurea', as a tree for quite small gardens. It is sometimes employed for hedge making, generally under another name, and it is quite effective for this purpose, being well armed and, as a hedge, not quite so depressing when used at some length as the purple plum. Grown as a short, standard tree it makes a compact, fairly-open head with small leaves, which two factors and the deep bronze rather than maroon foliage result in a generally lighter habit and tone than the purple plums.

One of the newer hybrids, *P.* 'Trailblazer', which has *P. cerasifera* 'Nigra' as one of its parents, inherits somewhat similar foliage. Its plenteous display of white blossom is often followed by a crop of small edible plums.

Much use is made of the purple-leaved crabs, as much for their gorgeous flowers as for their purplish-green foliage. It is always difficult to decide whether to choose *Malus* 'Alden-hamensis', *M. x purpurea*, *M.* 'Lemoinei', or the newer *M.* 'Profusion'—indeed, there is a great deal of similarity between them in foliage and flowers, and not a lot of variation in habit.

They are splendid trees in the right setting, not very appropriate in the broader scene but much sought after for more cultivated surroundings.

The purple-leaf birch, *Betula pendula* 'Purpurea' is worthy of mention. It is not a particularly vigorous tree, neither does it loudly proclaim itself, but its purplish-green foliage can often be used with very telling effect.

The copper and the purple beech really need no describing or extolling. They stand out as trees of major proportions with rich foliage tones and add a great deal to the landscape and large garden. The name *Fagus sylvatica atropurpurea* covers the various copper and purple beeches. 'Cuprea' and 'Purpurea', also 'Riversii' ('River's Purple') with large, deep purple leaves are clones of deeper coloration. 'Purpurea' has a weeping form 'Purpurea Pendula' which makes a most desirable tree.

Another tree which contributes much to the landscape is the purple sycamore, *Acer pseudoplatanus* 'Atropurpureum'. The colour is really confined to the undersurfaces of the leaves and is most telling when under a tree and looking upwards, or when the leaves are rippling in the wind. Even at a distance and on a still day the coloration is much in evidence for it does seem to permeate through and impart a purplish sheen to the whole tree, making it blend in with ordinary green tones rather than stand out as with the beeches and purple plums.

The Norway maple, *A. platanoides*, vies with the beech and plum in having a form or forms equally as deep in tone. Some term it 'Goldsworth Purple', some 'Crimson King', while others claim there is a difference in that either one or the other is the deeper of the two. Initially this is a tree which seems to take a little time to get going after planting and once it does is inclined in the early years to be open in habit with a tendency for some of the branches to stretch strongly sideways and produce a lop-sided effect. A little cutting back here and there until a shapely head is developing is often necessary.

'Purple' Shrubs

The glorious red tones in varying shades of the Japanese maples are preceded during the summer months by several with permanently maroon foliage, usually represented in gardens by either *A. palmatum* 'Atropurpureum' or *A. p. dissectum* 'Atropurpureum'. The first named has the typically palmately-lobed leaves of the type and is of deep, uniform hue. I have found this to come very true from seeds, few of the seedlings reverting to the green of the type with some variation in intensity of colour of the remainder, the majority being as deep in tone as the parent. *Dissectum* 'Atropurpureum' is generally seen as a fairly low-growing, rather spreading shrub and is a great asset as a specimen in a lawn or associated with suitable low-growing companions such as heaths. Its finely-divided foliage is not quite so strongly or uniformly coloured as the first named but it has an elegance which few other shrubs or small trees can match.

Many regret the substitution of the somewhat unwieldy name of *Cotinus coggygria* for the quite deservedly popular Venetian sumach or smoke tree formerly known as *Rhus cotinus*. There are several cultivars with foliage of a deep crimson to maroon shade, among which probably the deepest tone is displayed by 'Royal Purple', a strong-growing, somewhat spreading and most striking shrub. With a ceiling of 12ft or more it is a subject designed to enhance the larger garden or landscape rather than the average home garden. So, too, is the purple-leaf filbert, *Corylus maxima* 'Purpurea', which seldom seems to be used in sufficient quantity to pall and which can be extremely useful to give colour variation in the background.

Of more recent vintage, *Prunus* 'Cistena', sometimes called 'Crimson Dwarf', is a shrubby plum reaching about 4ft in height. With foliage akin to *P. cerasifera* 'Nigra' it is a very colourful subject and, likewise, must be used in digestible doses as an occasional group or a low hedge. Possibly, for very small gardens, shrub borders or formal lay-outs it could be grown as a short standard in much the same way as practised with forsythias, *Hydrangea paniculata* and certain other shrubs, and be quite an effective feature when in proportion to its surrounds.

The most popular of all foliage shrubs of this hue must surely be *Berberis thunbergii atropurpurea*. Sometimes one fears that popularity and familiarity will eventually breed contempt, something which has happened to more than one erstwhile species. This would be a pity for it is a shrub of distinction and of considerable value when properly used. Like its parent it is of modest growth and compact habit, not particularly outstanding in flower or fruit because of the more dominant hue of the leaves but, throughout the summer, it remains a uniform maroon to be tastefully employed. Fringe it with a silver-grey dwarf shrub or with the grey foliage and white flowers of *Anaphalis* and its value will be enhanced.

B. x *ottawensis* 'Superba' (*B.* *thunbergii* 'Atropurpurea Superba') has somewhat larger leaves of slightly deeper coloration with perhaps a stiffer, more upright habit. 'Atropurpurea Nana', which is synonymous with 'Little Favourite', is a very dwarf form of *B. thunbergii*, growing little more than 2ft in height and with many uses. My first, close up, impression of *B. t.* 'Rose Glow' was not very favourable, but at a distance I must concede that this is quite striking with its pinkish-red, young foliage flecked with silver and deepening with age to purplish-maroon.

Although rather duller than most subjects which have gone before I would still find a place if possible for *Weigela* (*Diervilla*) *florida* 'Foliis Purpureis' for it is comparatively slow growing and compact and not at all displeasing in foliage tone. Even the pink flowers blend tastefully with the purplish-green foliage. Perhaps of rather more widespread use and attraction is *Rosa rubrifolia* which is really unique among roses with leaves of purplish sheen, offset by the reddish-brown bark, to which can be added pink flowers and red hips of great value in their own right. Grown as a bush it has an open, pleasing habit; as a tall, informal hedge it is quite superb and never boring although, being almost unarmed it cannot be guaranteed to deter the invader quite like most roses used for this purpose.

Fuchsia magellanica 'Versicolor' is quite a delightful shrub with foliage one finds rather difficult to describe adequately, there being shades of greyish-green with pink and more than a hint of crimson and silver. Its cultivar name may appear as 'Tricolor'.

Then we turn to another 'Tricolor', this time a variant of *Hypericum* x *moseranum*, the offspring of a marriage between those two erstwhile species *calycinum* and *patulum*. The hybrid itself is a splendid low growing, 18in high, shrub which is evergreen except that in a severe winter, like *calycinum*, it may be cut to the ground but soon renews itself. 'Tricolor' has leaves edged with reddish-rose and flaked with silver—really, I suppose, this and the fuchsia could be classed as variegated—a pretty combination which never seems to pall or even in a mass become heavy and oppressive.

The grey-green leaves of the common sage, *Salvia officinalis*, have aesthetic as well as culinary value. Even more so its form 'Purpurascens' whose foliage, suffused with reddish-purple, can contribute to the effectiveness of any shrub or herbaceous border, even if it is not quite as hardy as the type. Its purple flowers are welcome but it is as a foliage plant and a foil to other more brightly coloured subjects where its true value lies.

The New Zealand flax, *Phormium tenax*, a plant of considerable character, of which more later, has a form 'Purpureum' with purplish-bronze leaves, but sadly this is somewhat tender as is *Pittosporum tenuifolium* 'Purpureum'. How valuable evergreens of this dusky hue are for winter effect in places which normally escape the searing effects of severe frosts and bitter winds, and what a pity more are not available for more general planting.

Hebe 'Bowles Hybrid' is a sheen of purplish-bronze throughout the summer and the bronze tints of the spring foliage of *Hypericum androsaemum* and *Corylopsis pauciflora* are maintained as long as growth continues. *Clerodendron bungei* (*C. foetidum*) has purplish staining in the young leaves to add to the purple of the stems and *Cistus x corbariensis* has foliage suffused with purple.

Hardy Plants and Carpeters

Among non-woody plants *Lobelia fulgens* stands supreme for the rich maroon of its foliage and for the brilliance of its scarlet flowers. It is at its best in the moist ground by the waterside but is not credited with being long lived unless lifted and given cold frame protection each winter—the usual practice when it is used for formal summer floral displays. Nevertheless, it can usually be counted upon to survive most winters,

Ligularias: formerly *Senecio,* the ligularias make impressive foliage and flowering plants for moist ground.

particularly if the crowns have a little protective material heaped over them, and the clumps are all the more effective when undisturbed and allowed to multiply.

Ideal for a situation by the waterside for it must have moist ground, *Ligularia dentata*, perhaps better known as *Senecio clivorum*, is one of those imposing plants we shall be looking at later. It has a most outstanding coloured foliage cultivar in 'Desdemona' whose young leaves start off the season in rich, purplish-maroon hue which becomes rather more absorbed into the green as the leaves develop whilst remaining an intense, deep colour beneath throughout their life. Making an upright plant some 4ft in height, one gets more than a passing glance of this rich coloration and when the stem terminates with orange flowers the whole plant is a most striking feature.

To lawn lovers and those beset by waste places the name plantain is ominous but there is a cultivated form, *Plantago major rubrifolia* which has leaves which compare in size with the weed itself in its most luscious form and not restricted to flattened rosettes as when a component of a lawn. These may be 6-7in long and are of a rich deep maroon colour. This is, of course, essentially a plant for the natural parts of the garden or waterside.

Sedums vary considerably in form and stature. *S. maximum* 'Atropurpureum', now regarded as a sub-species of *S. telephium*, is a most striking plant with its 18in stems and leaves of reddish-purple to offset the pale pink flowers. Although it is not really appropriate to mention it here I must pay tribute to *S.* 'Autumn Joy' ('Herbstfreude'), not for the munificence of the rose-pink flowers, beloved by bees, in their rightful season which comprises several weeks from late summer onwards, but for the deep crimson to which these flat heads gradually pass, with the leaves and stems turning brown and lasting in this pleasant warm tone for most of the winter. These, of course, can only be enjoyed in those gardens where the urge to cut everything down and clean up after leaf fall is stifled.

The hybrid between *S. cauticola* and *S.* 'Autumn Joy' called 'Ruby Glow' is only about half the height of the latter and is a valuable short plant for the front of the border with its purplish-grey leaves and rich ruby-red flowers. By comparison *S. middendorfianum* is a mere dwarf, being no more than 6in high, with golden flowers over a carpet of foliage which gradually turns to purplish-red as the summer advances.

As with the sedums generally, there is a wide choice of houseleeks, *Sempervivum*, but there is much less variation in form and stature. Essentially plants for the rock garden, dry wall or paving their rosettes of fleshy leaves are always compelling. This is especially so when they are tipped with red or bronze, or wholly of this colour—and there is considerable variation in the extent and depth of this coloration to form happy contrasts with the totally green or greyish-green forms when planted in colonies.

In distinct contrast to the heavier form and foliage of the sedums and sempervivums are the finely divided leaves of *Foeniculum vulgare* 'Purpureum', that purplish form of the common fennel, a pot-herb of bygone days. In sun or partial shade the upstanding stems so clothed impart a welcome feathery picture which is a delight also as a source of foliage for the flower arranger.

Any plant which waits patiently, but attractively, all summer to flower in early October is worthy of some acclaim for flowers are beginning to get rare at that season, particularly in the cooler, shady conditions in which *Saxifraga fortunei* delights. This is not an under-rated plant but it is seen all too seldom. It tends to make an early start in spring and its young fleshy leaves may get badly nipped by late frosts but it soon starts off again quite undeterred. Again in the autumn the branching stems of small, white flowers are liable to be spoilt by early frosts, but the risk is well worth taking for always there is the foliage to delight throughout the summer months. Glossy green on top, it is the under surface which is coloured crimson-maroon, deeper in 'Wada's Variety' where the colour seeps through to the upper surface.

Some plants are colonisers by their ability to spread and root laterally, others by prolific seeding and germination. *Viola labradorica* comes into both categories but perhaps it is by seeding that it is most likely to wander afield, the seedlings often springing up quite some distance away from the parent plants. This habit need cause no alarm for, caught before they have time to become fully established and take their turn at seeding, unwanted plants are not difficult to destroy. The leaves are thoroughly permeated with deep purplish-maroon to such a degree that with the young leaves there is little trace of green. Naturally the lavender-mauve flowers do not show up too well against such foliage but are an added attraction, although unfortunately quite scentless. Sun or shade suits but it is best in sun and a light soil to intensify the colour of the foliage.

The maximum of light also brings out the best coloration in *Ajuga reptans* 'Atropurpureum' which becomes intensely maroon-purple under such conditions, less so in shade although here it has similar value as a low, ground cover. The bluish-purple flowers are an early summer bonus but it is a thousand pities that all the older foliage has shrivelled up by the time spring arrives for otherwise it would constitute a delightful foil for many small bulbs. The waiting young growths do, however, usually provide sufficient evidence of a purplish carpet to make it worth while interplanting, if mainly to provide a summer blanket for the bulbs. The fully clothed carpet can be used with telling effect in association with other plants, or beneath and fronting shrubs, particularly those with silver foliage. 'Multicolor' ('Rainbow') as its name implies is a mixture of foliage colours—green, red, bronze and yellow—but, basically, the deeper red prevails to give the general impression.

Acaena microphylla, one of the New Zealand burrs, is an even closer carpeter with bronzy-green leaves and is extremely valuable for a sunny position on the rock garden or dry wall where its gradually extending mats and ability to percolate along and root well into any crack or crevice will not cause consternation. For a niche in paving it is eminently suitable for it is wiry and can be trodden on occasionally without suffering much damage. *A. inermis*, sometimes regarded as a form of *A. microphylla*, has rather larger leaves and does not make quite such a low mat but is a splendid bronze-green carpeter and spreader.

That the purple clover, *Trifolium repens* 'Purpurascens' is not more widely advocated and used for ground cover is rather surprising. Like the wild white clover it is a spreader but there is always a place for anything which goes on and on forming a close mat, particularly when it is of an attractive tone of bronze-purple. The lucky four-leaved form is probably the most interesting.

The creeping underground stems of *Houttuynia cordata* enable its foot high stems to clothe the ground especially if it is moist and the situation shady, and its heart-shaped leaves, at first green then blotched with deep maroon which gradually pervades the whole, are a perfect base for the small white bracts which surround the flowers.

At 4ft high *Euphorbia sikkimensis* is one of the taller of the herbaceous spurges. Starting off with rich red young shoots and leaves these gradually turn to green but the leaves retain this bright red along the centre veins and along the edges to give an effect like a smouldering fire beneath the heads of yellow bracts produced during the summer.

Parochetus communis may enchant with its delightful blue pea-like flowers produced in succession during the winter although liable to be damaged by frost but for compensation there is the worth of its close spreading mats of clover-like foliage, each individual leaflet marked with a conspicuous purplish-brown zig-zag line.

Geranium punctatum (the species I have which could be a form of *G. phaeum*) is one of a number of clump forming species invaluable for ground cover in shady places. Its deep green, quite large leaves have conspicuous maroon blotches in the crutches of the main lobes with smaller ones to set off the secondary lobes.

The narrow, sword-like leaves of *Carex buchananii* are brown and when seen for the first time one can be excused for wondering if they are dead, but this is quite a natural phenomenon and they do add variation to the waterside where this rather unusual sedge naturally thrives. Always for the foliage conscious there is something to be admired outside that which proclaims itself by depth of colour, grace or majesty of form.

CHAPTER SEVEN

Form and Texture

COLOUR ALONE, whether it be green in its divers shades or the wealth of other hues provided by both flowers and foliage, is but part of the picture. Without form, which most of us can interpret and appreciate, and without texture, that structural impression more difficult to define, a garden, no matter how rich and harmonious in colour could become a meaningless homogeneous mass very much devoid of character.

Like human beings some plants exude character in their general outline and bearing. Form and foliage almost invariably play the leading roles, flowers may be the culminating highlight, be of no significance or even, for a time, rather a detraction.

It is fitting to start with one of the largest leaved plants to be seen in gardens, *Gunnera manicata*. To say that a person of more than average height can stand up under a single leaf is no exaggeration for individually this may tower on a stalk up to 8ft long with a blade as much as 6ft across. This colossal amount of growth is all produced in one season for the plant is herbaceous. No other plant has a more imposing character. Even the great flue-brush-like flower spikes, although 3ft or more in length, can do no more than nestle in the crowns. Such giants, of course, need space, not only for their own curtilage but to enable them to create an impression on the landscape, in particular the margins of ornamental lakes where their character is displayed to the full.

Here, too, is the place for the giant rhubarbs, *Rheum palmatum*, and *R. officinale*, at around 6ft much lesser giants by comparison. Great, deeply-lobed leaves make the first impact, then these are surmounted by spreading panicles of creamy-white flowers which add to the overall effect. *R. palmatum* has several forms, *tanguticum* with larger and more deeply lobed leaves, *atrosanguineum* which adds a reddish tone to the under surfaces and is red flowered.

Still by the waterside, or at least where there is an ever-present underground source of moisture, such as a boggy area or a ditch which never completely dries, the 2-3ft elongated ovate leaves of the lysichitums make their mark

Gunnera manicata: massive leaves with ferns and *Lysichitum* in the foreground and backed with bamboos.

when the large arum-like spathes which precede them, yellow
with *L. americanum* and white with *L. camtschatcense*, have
likewise created an unforgettable impression.

Companions for the waterside, the ligularias all have leaves
well above the normal in size which have even more character
than the great heads of yellow or orange flowers in mid summer.
L. dentata (*Senecio clivorum*), *L. wilsoniana* and *L. veitchiana* all
have imposing heart-shaped leaves, the largest well over a
foot across, while those of *L. japonica* are deeply palmately
lobed. The plant generally cultivated as *L. przwalskii* is *L.
stenocephala* and is very distinct from the other ligularias,
being more spiky in habit and inflorescence and with purplish
stems. This colour extends into the main veins of the leaves,
which are rather smaller than the other species and very
deeply cut to appear star-like in shape. Sun or part shade suits
these ligularias; a situation where there is some respite from
the midday sun is favourite for even in the presence of adequate
moisture the large, rather-soft leaves may flag appreciably
during the hottest part of the day.

Generally *Rumex* spells trouble for this rather weedy genus
contains docks and sorrels but we must make exception
of the great water dock, *R. hydrolapathum*, with its 1-2ft broad
dark green leaves fading away in crimson shades in the
autumn, making a distinctive plant for the fringes of a major
water feature.

One mentions the giant hogweed, *Heracleum mantegazzianum*,
with some trepidation for it has received a great deal of
adverse publicity as a plant with extreme irritant properties
in its sap and from the hairs which clothe the stems and leaves.
Yet, given a place in a garden or, better still, in the landscape
where its large hollow flower stems are not accessible to
children, and with care in handling by those with sensitive
skins, it can contribute a great deal. Not only is it a plant of
major overall proportions—its flowering stems with great

flat plates of white flowers frequently attain more than 10ft in height—but its deeply cut leaves may be as much as 3ft long. There is added character in the coppery-red striations of the generously proportioned flower stems. Inclined to be mono-carpic, its capacity to renew itself by self-sown seedlings and its tendency to become prodigal in the wild along publicly accessible river and canal banks, no doubt spread by water-borne seeds, has contributed to defamation of character.

Angelica archangelica is another monocarpic umbellifer of prepossessing appearance. The large, much-divided, bright-green leaves on a luxuriant, tall plant can be used to fill an odd corner away from the more cultivated parts of the garden.

By comparison the rodgersias are genteel. They love a moist, peaty soil and thrive in sun or partial shade, being ideal plants for the fringes of woodlands and the waterside. *R. aesculifolia* has the largest leaves, the basal ones being 15-18in across. *R. pinnata* and its forms, differing from the type mainly in the colour of the quite beautiful panicles of foamy flowers which may be white or shades of pink and red, is probably one of the most popular. *R. podophylla* and *R. sambucifolia* are also imposing in herbage and have creamy-yellow and white flowers respectively. In contrast to the foregoing which all have very deeply divided, bronze-tinted leaves, those of *R. tabularis* are. peltate and a deep and satisfying shining green which is an admirable foil for the panicles of astilbe-like white flowers.

Morina longifolia and *Onopordon acanthium* have one thing in common, their thistle-like leaves, and there the connection ends. The *Onopordon* has already had a hearing as a silvery plant of distinction but I must add a rider for its considerable architectural value. *Morina* does not push up the same towering flower spikes and is content to distribute its forces with a number of 2-3ft stems from a rosette of 12in or longer, pinnatafid, spiny, evergreen leaves. As a flowering plant it is most interesting. The flowers are produced in dense whorls, intermittently and not all at once in each whorl, being at first white then gradually turning to pale pink and later to crimson when their job is done.

All the commonly-grown mulleins have character of form with imposing foliage, both best displayed where there is some shelter from strong winds which rather tend to disarray the tapering flowering stems. None is more impressive than *Verbascum bombyciferum* (*V. broussa*) whose large, woolly leaves have already been singled out for attention.

Among the meconopsis there are several which combine extreme floral beauty with foliage of distinction, particularly *M. regia* whose leaves are silver or golden haired and pinnately lobed. The great, flat, basal crowns are a most impressive sight during the winter months and continue to be so even when the tall, strong, flowering stems carrying similar, but smaller, leaves begin their upward passage. Like many of the *Meconopsis* this species is monocarpic and young plants, which are readily raised from seeds, should always be available to replace those which die after flowering.

With an increasing tendency by the populace to regard eating out as a night out, and more epicurean tastes, the globe artichoke, *Cynara scolymus*, once the prerogative of the landed gentry, seems to be coming back into favour as a vegetable for all and sundry. It is difficult to understand why it has lurked so long in the background as a vegetable delicacy only, for its habit and its large pinnately-lobed leaves make it a magnificent specimen. This applies also to the cardoon, *C. cardunculus*, which has already received compliments for its silvery-grey foliage, as have the huge glaucous-grey leaves of the seakale, *Crambe maritima*. *C. cordifolia*, on the other hand, is much more green than the ordinary seakale but has equally-large and impressive cordate leaves from which arise huge panicles of foamy white flowers.

These giant, somewhat fleshy plants with thong-like questing roots are gross feeders and must have a pretty fat soil if they are to attain their true imposing stature. This, too is a requisite of *Acanthus*, popularly known as bear's breeches and a real architectural plant if ever there was one. Whether it be *A. mollis*, its more robust form *latifolius* or *A. spinosus* with its more deeply-cut, somewhat-spiny leaves, the plant exudes character, but even its handsome foliage takes second place when the 4-5ft erect spikes of purplish-pink with white flowers begin to open, while remaining just the right dressing. Once well established—and some light winter protection may be needed until this happy state is reached—massive, steadily-spreading clumps will result. They are of inestimable value for isolated group planting, preferably in full sun, where a personality plant is required to command attention.

Acanthus mollis: handsome shiny foliage and great spikes of flowers make the bear's breeches a real personality plant.

Inula brings visions of herbaceous borders but few would contemplate including the elecampane, *I. helenium*, a colossus of a plant compared with the popular border kinds. A more natural setting is the place for its upstanding form with large boat-shaped leaves, the radical ones stalked and the others clasping the 6ft flowering stems.

It is general form rather than the foliage alone which characterizes *Euphorbia characias* sub-spp. *wulfenii*. This evergreen, perennial herb is shrubby in appearance, making a mound 3-4ft high of many fleshy stems densely beset with bluish-green linear leaves surmounted in due course with large, heavy heads composed of yellowish-green bracts surrounding the inconspicuous flowers. These, on top of the heavy stems call for a position sheltered from strong winds but still in full sun. Even with this precaution the end of the flowering season usually leaves some untidy bushes with branches sprawling in all directions and character a little sullied. Being readily raised from cuttings and developing quickly it is well worthwhile replacing periodically with young stock for it is

Mahonia japonica: one of the most impressive evergreen shrubs with sweetly scented winter flowers.

during the period leading up to the first heavy flowering that
form of plant and texture is of the highest.

In every respect the mahonias are valuable shrubs, be it
M. aquifolium relegated to a ground covering role or the
towering majesty of species like *japonica*, *lomariifolia* and
bealei. Here there is form of a less regular order to which the
large, pinnate, spiny leaves contribute in full measure, with
an added bonus of racemes of deliciously scented flowers
during the winter. *M. japonica* and *M. bealei* are often distri-
buted under each other's names but can readily be distinguished
for the latter has shorter, rather more erect, racemes of
flowers.

Fatsia japonica (*Aralia sieboldii*) has long been with us, having
been introduced from Japan in 1838, yet it has never quite
attained the popularity and the place in gardens that it deserves.
The same cannot be said of its bi-generic hybrid with the
Irish ivy, *Hedera helix* 'Hibernica', which came into being
almost a century later and which now, under the duo name of
x *Fatshedera lizei*, is achieving some popularity as a house
plant, despite its hardiness and capacity inherited from its
parents to prosper in deep shade and under town conditions.
Both are excellent distinctive foliage plants, *Fatsia* in particular imparting a somewhat tropical effect with its large,
dark-green leaves, deeply palmately lobed. When it attains its
ultimate capacity it is a large shrub, by then becoming rather
solid in appearance and with great, branching panicles of
milky-white flowers in October and November, a season when
they cannot fail to stand out and command attention.

Long linear foliage radiating from a crown also introduces a
sub-tropical effect and those who are fortunate enough to
succeed in the open with *Cordyline australis* will be able to
use this to advantage in the right setting. Always, however,
there are the yuccas to fall back on, *Y. gloriosa* to rise up
gradually on a stocky stem, *Y. filamentosa* as a stemless clump
former and a more prolific flowerer, or *Y. recurvifolia* with its

short, occasionally branching stems, recurved leaves and considerable capacity to flourish in town conditions. Finally, the long sword-like, sheathing leaves of the New Zealand flax, *Phormium tenax*, rise to an eventual overall height of some 8-9ft and gradually spread sideways into a great erect clump to provide a most conspicuous feature when standing in isolation or towering above a lower growing groundwork. This completes an all too scanty picture of some of the plants which bring impact to a garden and landscape by their general bearing and the munificence of their foliage alone.

More Impressive Foliage

Turning now to others which, in a less forceful way, make their mark on the general picture we must give the plantain lilies pride of place. Green, glaucous or variegated, bold and outstanding as with *Hosta sieboldiana*, *H. ventricosa* and *H. undulata erromena*, or comparatively small and elegant as *H. lancifolia*, their place in practically any garden is assured, more particularly where shady places have to be clothed, provided always there is adequate moisture to bring out the best in them.

The hellebores too are a versatile race. They prefer some shade but tolerate sun; they like their fair share of soil moisture but despite this I have found the Lenten rose, *Helleborus orientalis*, take extremely kindly to the often arid, dappled shade of trees. Although we may plant *H. orientalis* more for its flowers it could be that its large, dark green, shining, deeply palmately divided, evergreen leaves will contribute more, certainly to the general character of the scene. The popular Christmas rose, *H. niger*, is less impressive in this respect but is not to be despised as a summer foliage plant—it pretty well dies down for the winter. In support we have the dark, shining-green of *H. foetidus* and the grey-green, prickly edged foliage of *H. argutifolius* (also known as *H. corsicus*), species which are at their most interesting best when surmounted by their valuable greenish winter flowers.

Whether growing as a large tract or a mere clump in a pretty moist spot *Peltiphyllum peltatum* (*Saxifraga peltata*) cannot fail to command more than a cursory glance. Broad corymbs (1-2ft) of pale-pink flowers on fleshy, hairy, red-tinted stalks in April, arising from fleshy, but tough, truncated surface rhizomes may be regarded as curious and interesting rather than beautiful. The round, bright, shining-green, crenately-lobed, peltate leaves as much as a foot or more across, on 1-2ft stiffly hairy stems make it aptly named the umbrella plant. Unlike so many herbaceous subjects there is an appreciable last fiery fling as its foliage approaches the end of its life.

Also known as the umbrella leaf, *Diphylleia cymosa* in many respects is quite a different plant. It has quite large radical leaves springing annually from a thick, creeping, short-jointed rhizome with foliage character of no mean order. In late May and June terminal cymes of silvery-white flowers are produced on stems above the main leaf formation and these are succeeded by deep-blue berries about three-eighths of an inch across. At the same time the peduncles take on reddish tints and so we have a plant which in foliage, flowers and fruit is alive with interest throughout the growing season, requiring only a humus-containing, moist soil and appreciating partial shade.

Podophyllum hexandrum (*P. emodi*) and the American mandrake, *P. peltatum*, have large peltate leaves but are by no means so prodigal of foliage as either of the foregoing, the first named annually pushing forth a pair only and *P. peltatum* a single leaf. *P. hexandrum* is the most attractive for the leaves are beautifully marbled. Both the foliage and the fleshy rootstock is poisonous but, strangely, the large, red, fleshy fruits which succeed the white flowers are edible and quite a feature in themselves. Both are plants for the shady woodland and moist peaty conditions.

Always one praises poisonous plants with a deal of circumspection but, unless continually accessible to children, if their dangerous traits are known they need not be black listed for the majority of gardens. There can be little danger in the poisonous rhizomes of *Veratrum nigrum* and *V. album*, respectively the black and the white hellebore, both foliage plants of more than ordinary interest and character. Splaying out sideways from strong 3-4ft stems the bright-green sheathing leaves are most conspicuously corrugated and remain the dominant feature of either species despite a measure of attraction in their blackish-purple or greenish-white flowers. Partial shade is desirable for in strong sun, particularly if the soil gets dry, the leaves may be disfigured by scorching round the edges.

Veratrum nigrum: the sheathing, corrugated leaves of the black hellebore have a character of their own.

Much foliage of intrinsic value is contained among the subjects grouped as culinary herbs whose savoury value in the kitchen is perhaps now showing some signs of a come back. By and large their worth as ornamental subjects centres around the aromatic virtues of a very high proportion of them, and this we shall be looking at later. For a certain majesty of foliage the old clary, *Salvia sclarea*, not to be confused with the garden strains of so-called claries which are in use for bedding purposes, although of a biennial nature could well be used as a short term subject in a perennial border where its great, hoary leaves and 3ft stems of lilac flowers contained in pink and white bracts will be both interesting and impressive. It may well be that the form *turkestanica*, known as the Vatican sage, will be preferred. This has white flowers and rose tinted bracts and stems.

Phlomis russeliana (*P. viscosa*) is quite distinct from the shrubby Jerusalem sage, *P. fruticosa*. It is an evergreen perennial herb with considerable architectural value by way of its large basal leaves, a pleasant green above, greyish-green beneath and all hairy and wrinkled. Generally some 10in long and 5in across, they are deeply heart-shaped at the base with crenate margins. When the strong, square-flowering stems begin to push up some of the value of the lower foliage may be hidden and it is then that the lover of quiet, floral beauty will delight in the successive, dense whorls of up to fifty flowers with hoods of fawn-yellow and lips of soft gold, a delicate and rather bewitching combination. The character of the plant is such that it can be used in a natural setting where, planted in depth, it will cope successfully with weeds, given an isolated position as a more focal point and yet not look out of place in the more regimented quarters of the flower border.

Telekia (*Buphthalmum*) *speciosa* too is a plant quite capable of performing a dual role. If placed in the flower border it should be well to the rear for it has a ceiling of around 5ft. Like *Phlomis*, with its large, hairy leaves and bold heads of orange-red flowers it really looks more at home in less formal surroundings and will just as effectively hold its own in the face of weed competition.

One stands in danger of being labelled a foliage fanatic to even suggest that paeonies have more value as foliage than as flowering plants. We have seen what they can put forth in the spring. When in flower they are undoubtedly eye catchers and while I, on the whole, may be unmoved by the majority of large, double, globular, highly coloured flowers, I am quite partial to most paeonies, particularly if they have a delicious, pervading fragrance. As floral glamour fades their foliage once more comes back into prominence, particularly that of the shrubby paeonies—which shows that form is often very acceptable even when shorn of its trappings and can help a great deal when the floral make-up has wilted away.

Often it is before flowering that the foliage has its heyday. *Anemone* x *hybrida*, better known as *A. japonica* or *A. hupehensis*, is one of our most valuable late summer flowering plants, which in the months preceding shows much foliage character. This applies to many plants grown almost exclusively for their flowers. Those, who are not foliage conscious to the extent of using it for itself alone, should at least endeavour to bridge some of the rather unsightly gaps which are always apt to appear in the floral array by making full and proper use of those species which are not stripped to the waist when their floral jewellery is not sparkling.

Finely-divided Foliage

Poise and substance needs some gracing with elegance. Many of the plants noted in preceding chapters have it although it may not always have received specific mention. Without retracing our steps let us pinpoint a few whose prime quality is elegance of foliage whatever the flower that may follow.

Among trees and shrubs the outstanding performers are *Acer palmatum dissectum* and its purple foliaged form. Split right down to the leaf stalk each leaf segment is again deeply lobed and toothed to form a lacework on a spreading, often irregular bush to be admired by one and all. Most of the trees and shrubs with pinnate leaves are full of grace but generally these are dealt with under other headings.

Among hardy plants there are the giant fennels, *Ferula*, and the true fennels, *Foeniculum*, the former generally plants of somewhat massive proportions and with which I am not very familiar. The once popular culinary herb, *Foeniculum vulgare*, is no weakling for it can attain 5ft in height and form a billowy patch of light green hazed with yellow, imparting feathery grace and providing a plentiful supply of cut foliage. Its purple-leaved form 'Purpureum' has already been singled out for colour.

Another once popular culinary herb, sweet cicely in household and *Myrrhis odorata* in botanical terms, like fennel can be put to aesthetic use. Quite apart from filmy foliage which is full of visual charm there are aromatic qualities to also seduce—but more of that anon. Dill, *Anethum graveolens*, another old pot herb with finely-divided leaves, although of annual character, could well be employed here and there as an ornamental filler.

Often one deplores the need to change established botanical names in the interests of scientific purism, especially those of native plants like the tansy, formerly *Tanacetum vulgare* and now officially *Chrysanthemum vulgare* which somehow does not sound quite right. Be that as it may this is another of the old herbs whose role in the garden has changed from a source of flavouring to ornamentation, although not employed as much as it deserves to be in the flower border. Apart from the flat corymbs of yellow flowers, which can hold their own with many similar composites, there is a freshness and a frilliness in the bright green, netlaced foliage of this upstanding plant.

The thalictrums generally have finely divided foliage, *dipterocarpum* and *aquilegiifolium* in particular. I think I prefer *dipterocarpum*, the taller of the two, for its foliage is rather more feathery and the flowers follow suit, being less densely concentrated than *aquilegiifolium*. These, of course, are plants for the flower border rather than the wilder parts of the garden.

Filipendula and *Astilbe* provide us with species and garden cultivars with elegant foliage but by far the most outstanding of all in the clan is the closely allied *Aruncus dioicus* (*A. sylvester*), formerly known as *Spiraea aruncus*, and in everyday language as goat's beard, a flowering plant of considerable distinction for sun or shade with plenty of moisture at its feet, and with foliage that has much to commend it. 'Kneiffii' is a dwarfer and more delicate version with leaves so finely divided that they are almost thread-like in appearance.

Dicentra formosa and its cultivars have previously been noted but they must also have a place here for the extreme value of their finely divided foliage, dwarf habit and ground clothing capacity, let alone their flowers. *Corydalis lutea* may abound in many gardens having established itself by seed in all sorts of cracks and crannies in rock gardens, dry walls and odd corners where it produces its yellow flowers in endless succession throughout the summer. Always, however, it is worth growing, perhaps with a little rigid control, for its daintiness of foliage and for its ground covering value in sun, or in the partial shade which it really prefers.

Ferns have never quite achieved the general popularity they so richly deserve. Without exception they are superb foliage plants, generally preferring the cooler, shady parts and reasonably moist, in some cases quite wet, soil conditions, although many will endure, if not actually relish, the drier soil beneath trees or even full sun. The majority have much divided foliage, none more elegant than the maidenhairs which are, unfortunately, not quite so robust as the majority. There are numerous species of these but only a few with any chance of longevity in the open garden. *Adiantum pedatum* with very

black stems and delicate fronds is likely to prove the hardiest
and in the more favoured districts where a cool, shady,
sheltered spot needs gracing it is well worth trying *A. venustum*
and *A. capillus-veneris*. Covering the crowns and rhizomes with
a mulch of leaves or bracken kept as dry as possible during
the winter will help to ensure survival.

Both the lady fern, *Athyrium filix-femina*, and the male fern,
Dryopteris filix-mas, can be counted on to augment the comparatively small band of plants which will thrive under the dry
shade of trees. Although perfectly hardy their dead fronds
should be allowed to remain throughout the winter. Indeed,
emulating nature by forgetting tidiness, they can with advantage
be left to rot down and mulch the plants.

The graceful ostrich fern, *Matteuccia struthiopteris* (*Struthiopteris* or *Onoclea germanica*), does require very moist conditions

Osmunda regalis: truly a royal fern at its majestic best by the waterside.

even to the point of being boggy. Because it has the unusual habit for ferns of producing slight stems it does tend to make a more upright, distinctive plant. The sensitive fern, *Onoclea sensibilis*, together with the majestic royal fern, *Osmunda regalis*, are also very much at home by the waterside, be it in sun or shade.

As they are evergreen the polystichums have a value of their own. The hard shield fern, *P. aculeatum*, and the soft shield fern, *P. setiferum*, and their forms, some of them crested, complete a very short perusal of a race of plants which could well be accorded a more honoured place in gardens and the wider areas than it usually enjoys. To walk through a glade of fresh green, cool bracken in the heat of a midsummer day is delightfully refreshing but this, of course, is one of the ferns we have some need to destroy rather than cultivate. Why not then provide an alternative, where space permits, or at least more often use ferns to furnish and turn the odd shady corner into a pleasantly cool retreat?

Character with Ground Cover

A close carpet of foliage where otherwise there would only be grass, weeds or bare earth in itself adds to the character of any garden but more so when we get away from vincas, *Hypericum calycinum* and ivies which, splendid accommodating plants and weed suppressors though they may be, and always pleasant to look upon, seldom make one pause awhile and admire.

Pachysandra terminalis and its variegated form also enjoy some monopoly but here there is rather more definable texture and character in the larger, shiny leaves. Bergenias, with their great, glossy, elephant's ears of leaves are, of course, quite superb but one would hardly use them on their own in great masses which would tend to destroy their individuality. Up to a point this is also true of that outstanding woodlander, *Trachystemon orientalis* which has to endure the synonyms of

Borago orientalis, *Psilostemon orientalis* and *Nordmannia cordifolia*. Generally committed to the shade but by no means averse to full sun, content with either moist or rather dry soil, it is a splendid ground coverer. The first signs of activity are attractive loose cymes of blue flowers springing from the bare earth in mid-March. Then follow the large, hoary, cordate to ovate leaves up to 12in long and 8in across. Although not completely above suspicion for its territorial ambitions it is not a particularly rapid or insidious forager, makes a splendid masser beneath large rhododendrons and other shrubs and, being deciduous and capable of thrusting through any applied mulch, does not interfere with such winter cultural operations where practised.

The nature and the appearance of the flowers of *Trachystemon*, and to some extent the foliage, bring to mind that beautiful menace, the winter heliotrope, *Petasites fragrans*. Generally the virtues of this plant as a ground coverer are cancelled out by its desire to trespass and take possession. But every plant has some place in nature if not in well tended gardens. To see *Petasites* clothing steep coastal cliffs to a foot depth with its large round, radical leaves, effectively shutting out all other non-woody natural colonisers makes one speculate on the possibilities of using it as an alternative to the interminable grass on the banks of railways and motorways. As an occupier of more civilised places I am afraid its room is usually preferable to its company.

There is also a measure of similarity in the large, glaucous-green leaves of the blood root, *Sanguinaria canadensis*, previously referred to. *Trachystemon*, *Petasites* and *Sanguinaria* are all deciduous and for an evergreen of similar form and capacity to populate waste ground or that beneath and between shrubs there is an admirable substitute in the dwarf comfrey, *Symphytum grandiflorum*. This too can be invasive but not outrageously so for it spreads steadily by surface runners, producing a close carpet of dark green roughly hairy leaves

adorned in spring with pretty little creamy-yellow tubular
flowers lightly tipped with red when in bud.

Many wild plants have improved forms which have been
accepted among the hierarchy of the garden. Such a plant is
the bistort, *Polygonum bistorta*, which in the form 'Superbum'
has acquired a good deal of quality. It needs to have plenty of
moisture and its combination of foliage and flowers makes it
ideal for the waterside, but it is equally at home in any
natural setting in full sun or, if circumstances demand, even
complete shade. The elongated, oval, radical leaves, sometimes
as much as 12in long, on stalks of similar length have a wavy,
bright-green lamina and soon converge into a solid mass
capable of quelling all but the strongest of weeds. The
pale-pink flowers produced in dense 2-3in cylindrical spikes
at the end of long wavering stems in late May have an appeal
of their own.

I have left until last the ground cover plant whose virtues
in this capacity I never grow tired of extolling. *Geranium
macrorrhizum* is accorded a three-star rating in this book. I
give it top marks for texture and general appearance over
foliage colour and aroma, qualities brought to light elsewhere.
Unlike the majority of the true hardy geraniums it is not
strictly herbaceous in character, its short woody stems keep
it permanently above ground and, when all but a tuft of the
youngest leaves have changed colour and fallen, provide a
splendid receiving base and container for small fallen tree
leaves which nourish and add to its considerable capacity to
smother weeds. But it is that dome or broader 15-18in high
canopy of bright green, lobed leaves, individually somewhat
ordinary but collectively displaying texture and class which
make it stand out from other plants serving a more utilitarian
purpose. And its flowers of a pretty pink shade, white in the
form *album*, do not, like so many geraniums of similar type,
strike upwards on elongated leafy stems to become untidy
when spent, but hover just above the foliage and are absorbed

by it as they fade.

Spiky Leaves and Grasses

Just a few species are worth singling out for the foliage character they impart. Others in this category have been mentioned elsewhere for the other foliage virtues they possess.

The kniphofias are invaluable in the herbaceous border for the spikiness of their linear leaves as well as for their red hot poker flowers. *Agapanthus campanulatus* (*A. umbellatus mooreanus*), with its long, dark, shiny leaves and umbels of glorious sky-blue flowers on long stems is hardy in the milder parts, can always have its crowns protected during the winter or, as a last resort, can be grown in tubs and given indoor quarters when dormant. We now have the 'Headbourne Hybrids' to give variation in floral tone.

Irises of various types, from the popular bearded forms of glaucous-green, *foetidissima*, *sibirica* and so on serve many parts of the garden with flowers and very acceptable foliage throughout the year or for their period above ground. The wandflower, *Dierama* (*Sparaxis*) *pulcherrimum*, also of the iris family, has rigid, grass-like foliage as a base to its 4-5ft arching stems carrying pendant bells of flowers in shades of pink to red and purple, both foliage and flower stems uplifting and adding grace to the flower border.

For more natural places and closer to the ground there are liliaceous foliage plants like *Liriope muscari* with its grass-like evergreen leaves from which arise the spikes of lilac flowers, and *Reineckia carnea*, a rather uncommon plant, also evergreen with very fragrant pale pink flowers in April followed by red berries.

Among ornamental grasses the silvery, glaucous and variegated forms rather predominate and these have been mentioned in other chapters. These and the comparatively few green species which are grown ornamentally for their foliage always provide a change of form from the usual run, especially that of the taller, less mat-forming species. That is why the pampas grass, *Cortaderia selloana* (*Gynerium argenteum*) makes such a splendid specimen plant in a lawn, with or without its great feathery plumes in the autumn. Truly this is the aristocrat of the great grass family.

Trees and Shrubs of Distinction

For those who are fortunate enough to be able to grow them outside, if one wishes to impart a sub-tropical effect there is nothing better than the Chusan or fan palm, *Trachycarpus fortunei* (*Chamaerops excelsa*) and *Cordyline australis*, often also referred to as a palm but a member of a quite different family. The great fan-shaped leaves of the *Trachycarpus*, often as much as 3-4ft across, and the crown of long, linear leaves of the *Cordyline* surmounting the slender but rigid trunk formed as the years pass by, are in distinct comparison and both, as isolated specimens, will stand out in a garden. Sometimes one feels they are in keeping only when a fair proportion of the supporting plants are likewise immigrants from much warmer climates—with an accompanying cast that is largely temperate they can sometimes be made to look out of place.

The Japanese angelica tree, *Aralia elata*, also is distinctly tropical in appearance but not so likely to be the odd one out in other company. We have looked at its variegated form and the remarks then made apply also to the green-foliaged type. The large pinnate leaves of the stag's horn sumach, *Rhus typhina*, together with the more finely divided ones of 'Laciniata', on a small tree or large suckering shrub of rather gaunt, spreading habit, always show to advantage, especially when the hairy, crimson clusters of fruits are formed on the ends of the branches of female plants.

Rejoicing in such names as the golden rain tree, China tree and pride of India, *Koelreuteria paniculata*, with its irregular branched habit is claimed to be the tree depicted on the original willow-pattern pictures. This in itself stakes a place for it as a subject of more than ordinary interest but, more important, the pinnate leaves, as much as 15in long, coupled with its rather picturesque habit, are qualifications for a place as a medium-sized tree or very large shrub in any fair-sized garden. There is a fastigiate form which, if it were not so rare, would bring this tree into the range suitable for more limited areas. Late summer, however, is its crowning glory for then it blazes forth with 12-15in terminal upright panicles of yellow flowers quickly followed, sometimes before the last of the panicles have faded, with bronzy conical three-valved, bladder-like fruit capsules. Finally it precedes leaf fall with golden tints—what more could one ask of any tree, and why, oh why, is it not more readily obtainable, for it does come quite easily and quickly from seeds?

Pinnate foliage always tends to impart a degree of elegance and when large there is renowned character also. The Caucasian wing-nut, *Pterocarya fraxinifolia* (*P. caucasica*), which is closely allied to the walnut, is a tree which can almost vie with *Aralia* for the splendour of its often 2ft leaves consisting of up to thirteen pairs of leaflets plus the terminal. Of a glossy deep green in colour they also have considerable autumn value and the tree as a whole, being a fast grower of major propor-- tions in good moist soil ought to be a godsend to those who wish to impart character with some speed. Yet, strangely enough, it seems to be almost a rarity.

The Indian bean, *Catalpa bignonioides*, whether in green or golden form, is a tree whose foliage is its prime asset, and although we may plant the tulip tree, *Liriodendron tulipifera*, where we have the space, primarily in the hope of subsequently enjoying its unusual tulip-like flowers—and we may have to wait a good many years for the first showing—the out of the ordinary lobed, square cut, bright-green leaves, so wonderful in autumnal array, make it worth planting for the foliage alone.

So, too with another member of the same family, *Magnolia*

grandiflora, a truly magnificent evergreen either when free standing or trained up a wall, with great, glossy leaves at all seasons and massive, white flowers produced on and off, a few at a time anywhere between July and September. Wall protection is usually given to another evergreen, the Japanese loquat, *Eriobotrya japonica*, which has much of the foliage majesty of *Magnolia grandiflora* except that the leaves are wrinkled rather than smooth.

One has to depend on a fairly warm summer followed by a not too severe winter to enjoy the large, upright terminal panicles of purple, foxglove-like flowers of *Paulownia tomentosa* (*P. imperialis*) which make this tree an object of admiration and not a little wonder in May and early June. This precocity is due to the habit of forming flower buds in the autumn and subjecting them to the rigours of winter. A sheltered site in the milder regions does, therefore, offer greater chances of enjoying the thrill of the flowers. There is, however, an assurance that, flowers or no flowers, there will be the leaves, ovate to shallowly lobed cordate in shape and anything up to 10in long, deep green and hairy above and more thickly felted beneath. It will be even more magnificent if, writing off flowers and tree-like stature, one treats it purely as a foliage shrub by stooling back almost to the base each year and permitting one or more strong young growths to develop. Group planted and treated thus it can be an outstanding feature in the right setting.

Populus lasiocarpa has more class than many of its genus and, around the 60ft mark, is by no means one of the largest. But the same cannot be said of its outsize leaves averaging around 10in long and 6-7in across and hailed with joy by ladies collecting skeletonised specimens after leaf fall.

Everyone appreciates the character of the large palmate leaves of the horsechestnuts and if unable to accept their massive proportions in the confines of the garden can always be consoled with the dwarf buck-eye, *Aesculus parviflora*, a

tall, suckering shrub of real value for its late summer flowers
and one which is not used half as much as it should be. Its
value is reduced if it is hemmed in by other shrubs. By the
same token, seen more often but not always allowed to
display its virtues to the full, *Sorbaria (Spiraea) aitchisonii* has
elegance and grace in its open, informal habit, its large
pinnate leaves and great branching panicles of white flowers in
the latter half of the summer. But all too often its character
and particularly the delights of its foliage, are lost when it is
treated as an ordinary, back of the border, subject rather than
according it a degree of isolation in natural surroundings.

Those with an eye for leaf texture acclaim *Viburnum
rhytidophyllum*; others less perceptive and eminently practical
may bewail its habit, more pronounced in some situations and
seasons, of so drooping its leaves that the whole of the plant
looks drought stricken. While the common laurel, *Prunus
laurocerasus*, may be consigned to background planting the
dwarfer, spreading, narrow-leaved forms 'Schipkaensis',
'Zabeliana' and the newer 'Otto Luyken' are being broadly and
widely planted—sometimes one feels in rather too liberal
doses—for their general texture as well as their ground
covering capacity.

The large, woolly leaves and bristly, hairy stems of *Hydrangea
sargentiana* (now considered a sub-spp. of *H. aspera*), the
oak-like foliage of *H. quercifolia*, the shining, dark-green of
camellias, the corrugations in the low dome of foliage of
Viburnum davidii—these are subjects which have something to
offer other than foliar colour alone. And of the climbing
shrubs, although its real hey-day is the autumn, there is none
with more summer character than that truly magnificent vine,
Vitis coignetiae, many of its rounded leaves being 10in or more
in diameter.

Happy are they who can appreciate foliage for its form and
texture alone. As I write I look out on a narrow shaded border
backed by trees and undergrowth which, although it is

forever seeking to spread out into the garden, gives privacy and background to a low planting of subjects chosen for the quality of their foliage. There is *Bergenia cordifolia* alongside a broad dome of *Geranium macrorrhizum*, then in succession the large spotted leaves of *Pulmonaria picta* (*P. saccharata*), the bright green of *Hosta lancifolia* and *Tellima grandiflora*, the more filmy steely blue of *Dicentra* 'Adrian Bloom', the grey-green of *Alchemilla mollis*, and finally, in a broad nose pushing out into the sun for part of the day, *Brunnera macrophylla* interplanted with *Euphorbia epithymoides* (*E. polychroma*) for spring floral effect. One never tires of looking out the window at this narrow restful strip where flowers play an insignificant role but for the whole of the summer there is character, interest and serenity in the foliage alone.

CHAPTER EIGHT

The Indispensable Conifers

ALMOST WITHOUT EXCEPTION, the members of the great race of conifers are indispensable for their foliage in the landscape or garden. Foliage which is, a few genera apart, of an ever-green nature and thus doubly valuable. Indeed, it is true to say that without conifers the winter scene would sport only the odd evergreen, hardwood tree, generally an evergreen oak. Then there is the joy of the resinous aroma of conifers generally and the rich fruity odour of thujas when these are handled or brushed against.

Outline too is an outstanding feature. Where else can one find strictly pyramidal or narrowly columnar trees in such abundance, or species which are represented also by true miniature forms to impart the character of their parents in proportion to the rock garden, the heath garden and other scaled down representations of nature? Then there is foliage colour, from silvery blue-green through intermediate shades to dark blue-green, from real gold through yellowish-green to golden and silver variegations, and from soft pea-green through bright greens to the more sombre dark greens which tend to predominate, especially where grown for profit rather than appearance.

So wide is the range and choice that, together with the

knowledge that there are still quite a lot of discrepancies in nomenclature, I feel I must generalise and confine my thoughts mainly to a few which are in fairly-wide circulation and have more or less established names, rather than attempt to probe into depths I have not, as yet, fully explored. Indeed, one really has to be a specialist to write authoritatively about conifers at all.

Taller Outlines

Ultimate height and its fulfilment may be a matter of a good many or a comparatively few years according to the rate of growth of the individual species or cultivar, and differences can be considerable. So let us regard this section as covering those which will attain 15-20ft in reasonably quick time and go on from there according to their capacity. In short, species and cultivars suitable mainly for the landscape or the more capacious garden but permissible in small numbers when suitably placed in areas of more modest proportions.

Dark greens there are in some volume, be it the towering spires of the incense cedar, *Calocedrus* (*Libocedrus*) *decurrens*, the graceful pyramids of the fast growing western hemlock, *Tsuga heterophylla*, the more irregular outline of the Scots and other pines, or the variable tones of the Lawson's cypress, *Chamaecyparis lawsoniana*, so prolific with cultivars of other shades and habits.

From the silvery-grey of the slender drooping needles of the Bhutan pine, *Pinus wallichiana*, we pass on to the silvery-blue of the blue spruce, *Picea pungens* 'Glauca', and the Spanish-fir, *Abies pinsapo* 'Glauca', the greyish blue-green of the Atlas cedar, *Cedrus atlantica* 'Glauca', and the conical *Cupressus glabra* (*C. arizonica*), through the rather darker blue-green of *Chamaecyparis lawsoniana* cultivars like 'Columnaris' and 'Grayswood Pillar' to the much planted, rather more vaguely blue-green 'Allumii' which tends to get a little corpulent and ragged at the base with age.

Light, rather more enlivening, green is provided by the deciduous swamp cypresses, *Taxodium distichum* and *T. ascendens*, by the common European larch and quick growing Japanese larch, *L. kaempferi* (*L. leptolepis*), and the particularly pleasing, feathery daintiness of the dawn redwood, *Metasequoia glyptostroboides*, that one time fossil genus which was rediscovered in Western China in 1947. In evergreen form this tone is provided by the bright green of *Chamaecyparis lawsoniana* 'Erecta' ('Erecta Viridis'), unfortunately apt to go gappy at the base with age, by the sweetly pungent glossy foliage of the western red cedar, *Thuja plicata* (*T. lobbii*) and its improved form 'Excelsa', and by *Chamaecyparis lawsoniana* 'Green Hedger' which seems to be superseding *Thuja plicata* as a hedging subject of high order and a splendid specimen tree in its own right.

Lawson's cypress has also given us quite a choice of good, intensely-golden forms in 'Lutea', 'Stewartii' and 'Lanei', with 'Grayswood Gold' of rather more feathery habit and the compact, probably dwarfer, 'Winston Churchill'. The Monterey cypress, *Cupressus macrocarpa*, so valuable as a shelter tree in coastal areas but somewhat susceptible to winter damage in the colder inland parts, has several golden forms of which 'Donard Gold' of good colour and quick conical growth is, in my experience, one of the hardiest and best coloured. The flat branchlets of *Thuja plicata* 'Zebrina' are so liberally banded with light yellow that they give an overall golden effect rather than one of variegation.

Many more foliage variants among the taller conifers are there for the choosing and this small cross section merely illustrates how enlightened selection and placing can provide a panorama of varied foliage colour, particularly during the winter when conifers stand out in splendid array among the leafless hardwoods.

Ground-hugging Species

With ground cover so much in vogue these, the junipers in particular, have come into their own as never before, but are sometimes planted in breadths so great or so frequent as to impart drabness and a surfeit of flatness. Nowhere is the elegant form of a really prostrate-growing juniper better displayed than when splaying out over a rock face or bank. As a colony to provide an appropriate flat feature in conjunction with modern building architecture, or planted in depth merely to serve the more utilitarian purpose of clothing the ground and suppressing weeds, it too often loses all its individuality. But we are not studying landscape architecture so much as plants so let us assume that whatever we choose it will be rightly placed and tastefully used.

Among the real ground huggers *Juniperus sabina tamariscifolia* is one of the most popular of the deep green sorts. For bluish-green foliage there is *J. horizontalis* 'Glauca' and the Waukegan juniper, *J. h.* 'Douglasii', both rather dwarfer than *tamariscifolia*. Both the common and the Chinese junipers, *communis* and *chinensis* respectively, have prostrate forms if one wishes to depart from the usual while achieving the same purpose.

The rather taller, spreading conifers are also good for ground cover but also ideal for adding form to a garden, especially when used as isolated specimens in a lawn. Here again the junipers rather tend to dominate with the strongly spreading, feathery, blue-green *J.* x *media* 'Hetzii', the glaucous-green *J. sabina* 'Tripartita', the quite-golden *J.* x *media* 'Plumosa Aurea' and x *media* 'Pfitzerana Aurea' whose feathery younger shoots start off a soft yellow which assumes a more bronzy tint in autumn and then reverts to yellowish-green for the winter.

Juniperus chinensis 'Variegata', a somewhat slow spreader, has its branchlets, sometimes whole young shoots, attractively tipped with creamy white. Or we can be content and very well served with the grey-green of *J.* x *media* 'Pfitzerana' and others which make wide spreading bushes.

The popular steely, blue-grey *J. squamata* 'Meyeri' is rather more bushy in form, ie height approximating to the spread. *Taxus baccata* 'Adpressa Variegata' ('Adpressa Aurea') and 'Washingtonii' are excellent golden, bushy forms of the English yew.

Quite distinct from the majority of cypresses generally to be found in gardens, *Chamaecyparis pisifera* 'Filifera' ultimately forms a large, dense, spreading bush with slender, whip-like, arching branchlets, the whole forming a graceful dome of grey-green foliage. 'Filifera Aurea' and 'Filifera Nana Aurea', delicately but not intensely golden, are very popular and desirable colour forms.

These are just a few of the species and cultivars which take us completely away from the pyramidal or very much upright types which tend to be predominant. Because of their almost complete lack of formality they provide a priceless change of outline beside serving other specific purposes. 'Filifera Nana'

Chamaecyparis pisifera 'Filifera Nana Aurea': a stocky but graceful dome of whip-like, arching branches.

and 'Filifera Nana Aurea' form dense dwarf hummocks and can be used with good effect on the larger rock garden.

Slow Growing Forms

Many a nursery or garden centre label as dwarf and suitable for the rock garden and similar purposes species of conifers which, although it may take a number of years, may in time grow much too large for the purpose for which they were originally acquired. Take the popular *Chamaecyparis lawsoniana* 'Ellwoodii' as a case in point. Too often it is labelled a dwarf but it will ultimately attain a size suitable only for a large rock garden or a specimen on a lawn. It is important, therefore, to be able to distinguish between those which are dwarf only in their earliest years and those which are true pygmies and may take the major part of a lifetime to reach any appreciable height or girth.

The grey-green 'Fletcheri' is another which is by no means the dwarf it is often labelled. Other slow growing *lawsoniana* cultivars, too numerous to delve deeply into, include 'Pottenii' with soft-green, lacy, partly-juvenile foliage, the golden-tipped 'Ellwood's Gold' and 'Fletcher's White' and 'Albospica' which are variegated with creamy white.

C. *pisifera* 'Boulevard' is quite outstanding for its steely-blue foliage and has become deservedly popular but again it is not a subject for the small rock garden, also *Thuja occidentalis* 'Rheingold' whose delightful gold reaches its peak of intensity during the dull days of winter. Both these two cultivars are quite indispensable at that or any time of the year and nowhere do they look better than when associated with heaths.

One of the most satisfying of all golden conifers is *Chamaecyparis obtusa* 'Crippsii'. Ultimately it will make quite a large, loosely-pyramidal tree and I have seen beautiful specimens 20ft and more in height. But to me it is even more delightful when, having lost any semblance of a leader, it develops into a more open, irregular bush with tiered branches of flattened sprays of golden, younger foliage seated on that which has mellowed to a light green with age, in outline striking a somewhat similar chord in the garden to the tracery of the branches of an old Scots pine. It is then that one can really see eye to eye with those inspired landscape designers and planters who have the art of selecting and introducing misshapen trees into their plantings to impart interest and character just in the right place. 'Tetragona Aurea' is a useful substitute if one desires a spreading bush of tiered branches with irregular outline, clad with small branchlets of golden, ferny foliage.

C. *pisifera* 'Squarrosa' eventually makes a large rounded bush or small tree and retains its soft, glaucous blue-green, juvenile foliage indefinitely, with 'Squarrosa Sulphurea' of paler sulphury hue. *Picea orientalis* 'Aurea' ('Aureospicata') is a quite fascinating small shrubby tree with creamy-yellow young shoots, deepening in tone as they develop, finally becoming green.

For a complete change of outline we can choose one of the slow-growing Scots pines such as *Pinus sylvestris* 'Watereri' ('Pumila') to provide the more informal touch in places where tall conifers, or conversely the real dwarfs, are out of keeping.

Dwarfs and Pygmies

Here again the numbers available are so great and continually being added to that I must confine myself to a small cross selection merely to illustrate their value as foliage plants, additional to what is, perhaps, their greatest charm, that of form and character so indispensable in relieving any tendency towards flatness on a rock or heath garden or other reproduction of nature in miniature.

In green, *Picea glauca albertiana* 'Conica' makes a perfect close pyramid, *Chamaecyparis lawsoniana* 'Minima Glauca' a dome of sea-green, for more rounded form there is C. *obtusa* 'Nana' and C. *pisifera* 'Nana', the latter with tiers of flattened sprays of foliage. *Pinus sylvestris* 'Beuvronensis' is a delightful miniature Scots pine.

Among those of bluish-grey hue *Juniperus communis* 'Compressa' is quite supreme with its closely-packed, slender columns which take a number of years to reach 2ft in height let alone go beyond. On the other hand, the newer *Chamaecyparis pisifera* 'Snow' makes a miniature, rounded, bluish-grey bush and has its young foliage tipped with white, while *C. lawsoniana* 'Pygmaea Argentea' is variegated and tipped with creamy white.

For golden shades there is the yellowish-green of the flattened upright branchlets of the dome-shaped *Thuja orientalis* 'Aurea Nana', the brighter gold of the cones of *T. plicata* 'Rogersii' and *Chamaecyparis lawsoniana* 'Minima Aurea' or the little flat-topped bushes of *C. pisifera* 'Plumosa Aurea Compacta' and 'Plumosa Compressa Aurea' whose younger foliage is soft yellow in spring and the early part of the summer.

A host of others await selection. Choice must be guided by expert knowledge if one is not to run the risk of raising babies which will grow too large for the cot.

Winter Apparel

Last but by no means least are those conifers which, having fully played their part in form and greenery during the growing season, assume rich tones of purple and bronze to warm up the winter scene.

Perhaps the most heart warming of all is that bushy, elegant form of the Japanese cedar, *Cryptomeria japonica*, appropriately named 'Elegans' which has permanently feathery juvenile foliage turning to a rich rusty red for the winter. Or there is a smaller edition called 'Elegans Nana' of more purplish tint while, even dwarfer, 'Globosa' has the same capacity to put on winter garments and its dwarf, rounded form makes it very suitable for the small rock garden.

Several thujas oblige in this way. *T. occidentalis* 'Ericoides' forms a dwarf cone of dark-green, juvenile foliage which changes to brown when the days shorten. Several other forms of this species likewise assume bronzed tints in varying depths of tone. *T. orientalis* 'Meldensis' changes from soft green to deep purple and 'Juniperoides' ('Decussata') from grey-green to a purplish tint. Both are fairly dwarf species ideal for the larger rock garden or for associating with heaths. *T. orientalis* 'Rosedalis' is a real chameleon, adorning its sea-green, juvenile foliage with light yellowish-green when summer growth starts, gradually changing to its normal shade and then to its winter hue of metallic purple.

Chamaecyparis cannot, of course, be denied. This genus seems to provide something for every purpose where conifers are employed. For winter coat it has produced the dwarf *C. thyoides* 'Ericoides' of soft green juvenile foliage turning to bronze-purple, and *C. obtusa* 'Pygmaea' of dwarf spreading form and bronzed winter tints.

The Waukegan juniper, *J. horizontalis* 'Douglasii', so valuable as a spreading, ground coverer, and several other forms of *J. horizontalis* become tinged with purple in winter to provide a contrast with others of its habit. The gold of *Thuja occidentalis* 'Rheingold' and several others of its hue are attractively burnished. But, changing face or not, the quieter, duller months of the year in the garden and landscape can be immeasurably lightened and made more warm and cosy by the enlightened use of conifers in their multitudinous array.

This chapter had to be written for any book on foliage would be quite incomplete without some reference to conifers. It is wholly inadequate to do anything like justice to the value of foliage assisted by form and adaptability which this great race provides for man's benefit and pleasure. Those well versed in horticulture will instantly feel that I have done no more than scratch the surface but perhaps they will accept that, because of the vastness of this section of the subject, I have had to be content with a small selection for the benefit of the less well initiated.

CHAPTER NINE

Aiding and Abetting Floral Colour

THE INSPIRED HORTICULTURIST likes his floral colour suitably
ameliorated with form and foliage and is seldom moved to
ecstatic admiration when he views great masses of garden
flowers set out in seasonal, formal array. He may express the
opinion that no great skill is required to raise, plant out and
thereafter cultivate, while acknowledging there is some art in
the blending of form and colour, influenced to some extent
by personal taste in the actual mixing of the cosmetics. Here
the choice and use of foliage plants can do much to soften and
blend vivid colours and reduce any garishness. Those who
look askance at this form of horticultural display, should not
overlook the fact that it appeals to many thousands of garden
and flower lovers who are not blessed with insight into the
finer arts and tend to see the greatest beauty in large and vivid
flowers. But, of course, only those who have to provide and
display for a much wider clientele than self and family circle
have to take the catholic tastes of the masses into consideration.

In seasonal bedding the part of foliage plants is three-fold.
(i) they may add even more colour; (ii) they will help to
soften the glare of yellow, orange and scarlet shades or liven
up dull crimsons and purples; and (iii) they will provide the
necessary media to separate colour combinations.

Golden and variegated foliage generally plays an enlivening role, green and dark crimson or maroon helps to tone down while silver can be used effectively for either purpose. Form also is important for in bedding more use can be made of foliage plants as specimens dotted among the flowers to give lift to the beds than their employment in the general ground-work. Some dwarf species are, however, ideal for edging beds of flowers to frame the picture whilst contributing to the overall effect.

Apart, perhaps, from *Arabis caucasica* (*albida*) 'Variegata' comparatively little use is made of foliage in the spring display in which wallflowers, polyanthus, *Myosotis* and double daisies predominate, aided and lifted out of a flat carpet by the skilful choice of bulbs, generally garden tulips of one group or another. That the choice of foliage plants is very strictly limited is not really surprising for, apart from plants of an evergreen nature there are comparatively few subjects of suitable texture and form which have attained adequate foliage when the short period of full floral colour holds the scene. We are, therefore, mainly concerned with foliage plants to go alongside antirrhinums, petunias, salvias, mari-golds, lobelia and the like which make the formal parts of a garden so colourful from June until summer wanes.

Specimen Foliage Plants

Generally these are required to attain 18in to around 3ft when in their prime. Many are perennials which need to be raised from cuttings or seed during the previous growing season in order to reach the requisite starting height when planted out. This means glass protection for several months, but this applies also to many of the flowering subjects, making this form of horticulture an expensive and time consuming pursuit—but we will leave the methods and economics and take a look at suitable subjects.

Silver is possibly the most valuable foliage colour to employ.

It can be associated with practically any floral hue. With pinks and blues delicate pastel combinations can be achieved and it is extremely valuable with colours such as magenta which are a little difficult and unfriendly. Strangely enough, deliberate combining of silver with yellow flowers is not widely practised yet very many such foliage plants themselves produce flowers of some shade of yellow.

Centaurea gymnocarpa makes an imposing specimen plant around 2ft high at the height of the season and for this purpose is best raised from seed annually as vegetatively propagated stock is liable to branch out and flower, spoiling the symmetry of the plant. *Artemisia arborescens* can readily be trained to a stake and kept in upright or pyramidal form, and most attractive it is with its divided silver foliage, attractive also in my experience to town pigeons and house sparrows when grown in towns. Indeed, I have found the town sparrow most partial to silver-foliaged plants in general, even entering glasshouses through the ventilators to disseminate them, yet out in the country it seems to have better things to do.

Trained as a pyramid or a standard the small ovate leaves of *Helichrysum rupestre* will blend in rather than contrast, being a less intensive silver than either of the foregoing. It can also be used as a grounding subject for interplanting and threading through the main components.

The glaucous grey of *Eucalyptus* is available, several species being suitable for the purpose. The most widely used are the blue gum, *E. globulus* and the near hardy cedar gum, *E. gunnii*. Both provide a loose pyramidal effect and can be associated with almost any plant. *E. gunnii* needs a rather longer growing time prior to planting out and is less likely than *E. globulus* to make over abundant growth and tower above its associates before the end of the season is close at hand. The small cordate leaves of the young plants are lighter in general outline than the other species and its own lanceolate adult foliage which is not usually produced until a height of some 6-7ft is attained, at which stage the plants are generally too large for formal work. After its first season *E. gunnii* can be potted up for use again the following year as larger specimens if these can be employed with advantage. Then when it has quite outgrown its purpose in formal work, provided the latitude is such that there is a good chance that it will succeed it can always go into the open garden, if only to be planted in a sheltered spot. It can be kept to bush form by annually cutting back the young growths in late summer and giving them glycerine treatment to preserve them for indoor winter decorations. Treated in this way the leaves become suffused with purple while retaining their glaucous bloom and are most effective among similarly treated copper beech foliage, dried flowers, grasses and the other odds and ends which go to make a winter pot-pourri.

Good silver variegated foliage is provided by *Abutilon* x *hybridum* 'Savitzii' which, generally, only attains 12-18in in height in the beds and is best used with quite dwarf ground-work. The popular *A. striatum* 'Thompsonii' is golden variegated, makes a compact graceful plant of some 2ft if about 9in high when planted out and can be used very effectively with most colours, in particular forming a delightful blend with mauve and yellow antirrhinums edged off with a dwarf, pale-yellow French marigold.

For a formal, medium-sized pyramidal contour the silvery, lemon-scented *Pelargonium crispum* 'Variegatum' can be very useful and needs only a bit of finger and thumb work of pinching back in its early stages to train it to the right shape and to keep it tidy thereafter. It fits in with practically any floral colour.

Unfortunately *Hebe* x *andersonii* 'Variegata' is not sufficiently hardy except in favoured localities for general garden purposes for it is a desirable evergreen shrub with quite large leaves liberally variegated with cream. It does, however, make an extremely useful standard plant for the flower beds or can be effectively employed as dwarf, bushy plants from cuttings

Euphorbia marginata: white-edged leaves and white bracts make this a useful plant for formal work and for cutting.

inserted the previous summer. Its long racemes of lavender flowers, which pale almost to white with age, although of less value than the foliage, can add to the overall effect.

Foliage fuchsias make excellent specimen plants for the beds when grown in standard or pyramidal form, especially those of rich-golden coloration, of which there are several. Young 18-24in high plants of *Cupressus macrocarpa* 'Donard Gold', which is quite easily raised from cuttings in a propagating frame, look fine when golden-green pyramidal form is desired. As with *Eucalyptus gunnii*, these can be potted up and used again or given a permanent site in the garden if they have become too large for the beds. Although not reckoned to be adapted to the colder districts 'Donard Gold' is rather tougher than is generally supposed away from the warmer coastal areas. I have known it to come unscathed through temperatures perilously close to zero the winter after being transferred from the beds to permanent outside quarters.

If one cares to go to the trouble of training the small-leaved variegated ivies up cane tripods to form short pyramids these likewise can be very effective where such formality and colour is desired. *Miscanthus sinensis* 'Variegatus' and 'Zebrinus', excellent tall variegated grasses for the open garden, can be split into small clumps just before growth commences and potted up for use as dot plants. The check of disturbance makes them dwarfer and less dominating and just right for graceful furnishing.

Euphorbia is a large and varied genus and can probably claim to have a plant for every purpose—trees, shrubs, perennial and annual herbs, down to persistent weeds, adapted for conditions varying from quite deep, cool shade to the intense heat of arid deserts. Snow-on-the-mountain, by which popular name the annual *E. marginata* is known, refers not to any natural habitat but to the white-edged leaves which become almost wholly white near the apex where they are surmounted by the white bracts surrounding the inconspicuous flowers. This all makes a most attractive plant about 2ft in height if it escapes the attention of the flower arranger of the family for whom it is choice material.

Purple foliage is commonly provided by *Perilla frutescens nankinensis* or its cut-leaved form 'Laciniata', both readily raised from seeds sown in the early part of the year. The colour is deep, uniform and maintained throughout the summer. This depth of tone together with the rather solid-looking leaves and close, upright form impart a somewhat heavy appearance and one which calls for sparing use in the larger beds, particularly as the plants tend to get rather gross before the season is at an end.

Much the same form, colour and texture is supplied by *Amaranthus melancholicus* 'Ruber', *A. salicifolius* and *A.* 'Molten Fire' but the genus has more recently given us several very highly coloured hybrids somewhat less vigorous in habit. There is 'Tricolor Splendens', rich crimson-red irregularly splashed with bronze and yellow, 'Pygmy Torch' a dwarf crimson and 'Flaming Fountain' with bright, flame-coloured foliage to prove that although flowers tend to dominate the scene foliage can also provide a blaze of colour. These multi-coloured hybrids are for those who like a measure of flashiness and gaudy, sub-tropical apparel, coupled with easy propagation from seeds. To avoid confusion I have not attempted to be botanically correct and have given them the names under which they usually appear in seed catalogues.

The red mountain spinach, *Atriplex hortensis rubra* is also easy from seeds. This is a red-leaved giant growing 4½ft or more in height and, consequently, with limited uses. It can be employed as a quick growing plant to screen temporarily an unsightly object but, like other plants of rapid succulent growth it falls prey to heavy rain and strong winds when approaching maximum growth and does tend to become untidy later in the season.

Coloured foliage forms of the castor oil plant, *Ricinus*

communis, likewise make considerable growth during the summer and are liable to get out of proportion to their bed-mates. 'Gibsonii' has large, palmately-lobed leaves of reddish-crimson coloration, their long stems throwing them out to form a spreading, open plant which can reach 3-4ft or more in good soil in the first season from seed. This is a plant of considerable character, quite different in outline from *Perilla*, *Amaranthus* and *Atriplex* and ideal for sub-tropical bedding.

Undoubtedly there are many situations where *Lobelia fulgens* 'Queen Victoria' can be permanently employed and used with effect in the open garden but it can also create a good impression when associated with annual plantings for its crimson foliage surmounted by brilliant scarlet flowers. Generally all that is necessary is to box up sufficient plants for stock purposes at the end of the summer, winter in a cold frame with some added protection in exceptionally severe weather, split into suitably sized plants and pot up in February. Plants of narrow outline result, to be used for interplanting suitable companions or grouped together to form wider spaced, more imposing clumps.

One does not often see the red-foliaged forms of *Cordyline* (*Dracaena*) *terminalis* employed in the open garden but they can be very impressively used in southern regions as dot plants among low-growing groundwork. They will, of course, grow on under glass into much taller plants on stems but this is a long business and generally it will be found best to employ them first when 1-1½ft in height, lifting at the end of the season, potting up for the winter and using again as larger plants the following year and subsequently scrapping them when they have got too large or careworn. The narrow-leaved forms like the all red 'Manouk Bey' are generally more satisfactory than those with broader leaves.

Cannas are favourites with some. Their imposing foliage, often very deeply coloured, and their rather flashy flowers do not always agree with the more orthodox bedding plants and they are best used in association with sub-tropical efforts. So too with the various variegated forms of maize, *Zea mays*, where height and large, sheathing, coloured leaves can be effectively employed.

Last, but by no means least, we turn to plants with ordinary green foliage. They provide no startling effects on their own nor as partners in colour combinations but at times are necessary to impart a steadying influence to glittering floral colour.

The annual summer cypress or burning bush, *Kochia scoparia culta* (*trichophylla*) is widely used for its neat, erect, but rather dense, habit and small, light-green foliage which turns deep purplish red in the autumn. 'Childsii' is strictly a synonym of the foregoing but probably used to cover good forms which are generally a little less vigorous and not so inclined to get gross and top heavy in late summer.

Of much more elegant outline when grown upon a single stem, *Jacaranda mimosifolia* has light-green, bi-pinnate feathery foliage ideal for imparting a measure of lightness and grace to solid colour. This is actually a half-hardy tree which is readily raised from seed and also desirable as a pot plant for the cool greenhouse or the home. So too with *Grevillea robusta*, the Australian silk oak, which in its native land is a tree of the largest size. This has long been established as a graceful, decorative, foliage plant when in its infancy and invaluable for conservatories and internal decorative work. Its services can be utilised in a similar role to *Jacaranda* in the summer garden.

Also a tree but with a much lower ceiling and with quite a different palm-like habit, *Cordyline australis* is hardy in the milder parts so needs no great heat to grow to a size capable of being used as a temporary occupant of flower beds, housing at the end of each season until its gradually elongating stem lifts the crown of long, strap-shaped leaves too high to be really appropriate for formal work of this nature. Then, if the climate gives it a chance it can, like *Cupressus macrocarpa*

'Donard Gold' and *Eucalyptus gunnii*, be found a permanent home in the open.

Dwarf Foliage Plants

Generally these are employed for edging beds and are often more telling than flowering plants in that they frame the picture and help to soften the main span of floral colour.

The intense silvery whiteness of *Senecio leucostachys* (*Centaurea candidissima*) and cultivars of *S. cineraria* like 'White Diamond', 'Hoar Frost' and 'Silver Dust' helps to create delightful effects with almost any floral colour. Of the cinerarias 'White Diamond' at around 2ft in its first season is the tallest and suitable for the largest beds but the newer 'Silver Dust' is little more than half that height and probably

Senecio cineraria 'Silver Dust': one of the dwarfest of the several cultivars much in demand for formal bedding.

the most useful of the trio. Although all are perennials they are readily and best raised from seed annually.

Chrysanthemum parthenium (*Pyrethrum parthenium*) grows about 1ft high in its first season and has finely divided silver-grey foliage. There are much dwarfer golden-leaved forms like 'Golden Moss' and 'Selaginoides' which make ideal edgings although they are rather apt to go a little green towards the end of the summer and when clouded over with their white flowers some of the effect of their foliage is lost unless these are removed. But, of course, one can on occasion deliberately plant for both.

Calocephalus (*Leucophyta*) *brownii* is an odd little shrub composed of thin, stiff stems with tiny leaves, the whole an intensely silvered network of twigs. It can be used as an edging, even for carpet bedding, or for lacing through quite dwarf floral groundwork.

Festuca glauca is quite superb as an edging for beds. Its glaucous-grey foliage is a fine modulator, it is uniform in height and tidy in appearance, the only attention required after planting is to trim off the flowering panicles when they appear as they detract from the neatness of the whole plant. For bedding purposes the plants are best lifted when the season is over, planted in a cold frame without breaking the clumps and split up into suitably sized pieces when planted out again. Similar treatment should be accorded the variegated cocksfoot grass, *Dactylis glomerata* 'Variegata', which is just a little taller than the *Festuca* and not quite so tidy but, nevertheless, makes a uniform continuous edging.

The many and extremely varied garden forms of *Coleus blumei* generally have but a short season when planted outside for the summer, soon beginning to look careworn. This, however, does not apply to 'Golden Ball' although one would not expect to find it employed to any degree away from the southernmost parts of the country. Easily overwintered, readily raised from cuttings, once outside it stays around the

9in high mark, has narrow, golden leaves and seldom attempts to garnish this attractive foliage with the dubious value of its flowers.

There is a foliage *Fuchsia* which I have known for years as 'Golden Gem' but, not being one of the ever-increasing band of devotees of these delightful plants I cannot vouch for the authenticity of this name. But I do know it as an extremely useful edging plant of the same calibre as the *Coleus* and with little inclination to flower and break the golden band when employed in this way.

Much use is made of ornamental beet as foliage plants for summer bedding but some of the strains are apt to get rather gross as the summer advances. The 'willow-leaved' type, as its name implies, has much narrower foliage and generally makes a more compact plant.

Although grown primarily for their freely produced and colourful flowers, among the many excellent garden cultivars of *Begonia semperflorens* there are several with quite deep bronze or red foliage. The scarlet-flowering 'Indian Maid', available in semi-dwarf averaging 9in, and very dwarf strains, and the rose-pink 'Carmen' led the way and are still available and well worth planting today despite an influx of new cultivars. Among the later introductions 'Lolita' (scarlet), 'Vodka' (salmon-scarlet), the white-flowered 'Whisky', 'Frosted Chocolate' and 'Karen', the taller white 'Cappuccino' and the newer Devil strain in scarlet, rose-pink and white are worthy of note. All make first-class bedding subjects for sun or partial shade, for warm and dry or wet and sunless summers, at least in the southern half of the country. They are also excellent as house plants, flowering without cessation throughout the whole of the year, naturally somewhat sparsely during the winter months.

The iresines are among the easiest of plants to raise from cuttings and are valuable foliage subjects for bedding purposes. Growing some 12-18in high, their height and spread can be regulated by pinching back. There are at least two good forms of *I. herbstii*—'Brilliantissima' with crimson foliage and 'Aureo Reticulata' which is green splashed with gold set off by reddish leaf stalks and principal veins. *I. lindenii* has much narrower, very deep crimson leaves and, allowed to grow unchecked, can be useful for dot planting small beds.

The closely related *Alternanthera* is mainly employed for carpet bedding but can be put to good use for edging normal flower beds. *A. amoena* and *A. ficoidea* and their cultivars are quite dwarf with *A. bettzickiana* and *A. versicolor* rather taller. Many of their cultivars have multi-hued foliage in which shades of purple, crimson, red, brown, bronze, rose-pink, orange, yellow and green are matched in various combinations.

The attraction of heliotrope is, of course, its flowers, particularly their scent which not even the daphnes, *Viburnum carlesii* and others high in the perfumery charts can match. To some the very dark purplish foliage of *Heliotropium* 'Marine' is attractive but I feel that this tends to nullify the violet-blue of the flowers and the whole can be rather dull unless relieved by silver, white or shades of yellow.

Zonal and Ivy-leaved Pelargoniums

Zonal pelargoniums or bedding geraniums have long been stalwarts in summer bedding displays, including those with ornamental foliage. To say that, silver-leaved cultivars apart, these foliage forms make a big impact either in overall effect or ameliorating role would, perhaps, be an overstatement. Many of them rather tend to fall between two stools in that neither in flower nor foliage are they sufficiently outstanding to make a major contribution. Indeed, one sometimes feels that flowering does tend to destroy the value of the foliage.

This is particularly so with those cultivars where zoning in bronze, chestnut or even darker tones is the highlight of the coloration. 'Mrs Quilter' (dwarf with pink flowers), 'Golden Harry Hieover' (vermilion), 'Salmon Hieover', 'Crystal

Palace Gem' (rose), 'Happy Thought' (crimson-red) and the golden tricolors 'Mrs Henry Cox' and 'Mrs Pollock' are all moderate in flowering either in quantity or the density of the trusses, yet all have most attractive foliage when this is viewed as a separate entity. Their effectiveness as foliage plants would be increased somewhat if the flowers were removed but this is seldom economically possible and they should, therefore, be used only as secondary plants, preferably to edge off more colourful subjects when dwarf enough for this purpose, and several of them are.

On the other hand the silvers can be most valuable as dual purpose plants either as the dominating feature of a bed or combined with some other contrasting or blending subject tracing its way through them, framing the picture, acting as a base coat or rising above it. 'Caroline Schmidt' with red flowers and the pink 'Mrs Parker' and 'Chelsea Gem' are popular cultivars. The combination of the rather hard-red flowers of the first named does not suit all tastes, the pinks generally being more acceptable, of which 'Chelsea Gem' is reasonably dwarf and less apt to grow leggy in wet summers.

One silver zonal pelargonium stands out on its own. It is the very dwarf 'Madame Salleron' which I believe to be the correct name for the form I have grown and employed as 'Dandy' and 'Mrs Stott'. Among these zonals there is much duplication of names generally, many, like 'Mrs Stott', being local and some quite erroneously used. This particular cultivar makes a neat tufted plant 8-9in high and a little more across, seldom flowers and forms a perfect silver-foil edging to beds.

'Verona' and others which have yellow or yellow-green leaves have their uses and some may find interest and a certain charm in the near black foliage with black zone of 'Salmon Black Vesuvius' and 'Red Black Vesuvius' but these are rather lacking in vigour for external work.

The cultivars mentioned by name are only a few of those which are widely known and commonly employed for bedding purposes. There are numerous others but not all have the capacity to flourish in problematic summers. Among the ivy-leaved pelargoniums, 'L'Elegante' with small, white-edged leaves and white, feathered, maroon flowers is quite a good cultivar for outdoor display, under which toughening conditions the white in the leaves becomes diffused with pink and mauve. There are several other ivy-leaved pelargoniums but the only other one with coloured foliage that I really know at all is 'Crocodile', an Australian introduction which has recently gained some recognition. It has rose-pink flowers and the names of 'Sussex Lace', 'Alligator', 'Fishnet' and 'White Mesh' which it also enjoys are indicative of the white veinous reticulation of the leaves. It has its attractions but I have only grown it as an indoor plant.

While we tend to look upon foliage as the basis of a garden, as that permanency which no flowers, however long lasting or repetitive, can ever provide, it can also play a temporary and quite important role to make short term plantings much more interesting and of better taste.

CHAPTER TEN

Aromatic Foliage

FRAGRANCE IS ALWAYS esteemed in a garden but seldom exploited as much as it deserves to be. Too often it is but a corollary to plants chosen for their flowers or foliage. Whenever it is present in either it imparts an air of enchantment and often creates more nostalgic memories than all the vivid colours, the delicate pastel shades or the gripping appreciation of form and texture.

Naturally one tends to associate fragrance in plants with flowers, a quality so many possess and one designed to captivate the attention of pollinating insects so that the kind may be perpetuated rather than seduce mankind. Floral scents generally are more varied and sweeter than the aromas of foliage which, in some cases, tend to be spicy or pungent. Generally, also, the scents of flowers are cast upon the air whereas that of foliage is only readily discernible when the leaves are brushed against or even crushed. This helps to offset any tendency towards pungency which, in small doses, may be enchanting but, when protracted, can become oppressive. This elusiveness of foliage aromas does, of course, add to the charms; to handle or brush the foliage of *Geranium macrorrhizum* and be regaled with its seductive, spicy fragrance clinging to the hands or clothing for some considerable time is another bewitching side of this quite invaluable plant.

Aromatic foliage can be used in either of two ways. One can bring such plants together and display them collectively in an aromatic garden, giving careful thought to their assembly and making full use of those with desirable flowers and other foliage attributes. Or one can disperse them throughout a garden in their appropriate quarters and settings, doing so

Perovskia atriplicifolia 'Blue Spire': grey-green aromatic foliage, whitish stems and blue flowers make this an all round shrub.

with intent and not haphazardly so that all their qualities fit in and they are brought within close reach of those who use the garden, never neglecting the opportunity to drop in the odd suitable plant where it is likely to be unintentionally brushed against. Remember also that, as with flowers, fragrance tends to be more intense as twilight falls, particularly if the evening be damp or sultry, so some in close proximity to the dwelling house is sure to be esteemed.

As so many aromatic plants are culinary or medicinal herbs, probably more of bygone days than the present era, a garden planted exclusively with such herbs is just another name for an aromatic garden and will have an added interest. Those without the space or urge to subdivide their gardens will derive just as much joy by introducing and dispersing aromas, savouring them individually and to the full without the danger of becoming nasally confused as one samples and collects one odour after another in a more concentrated pot-pourri.

The Great Labiate Family

Here we have the greatest contributor to the highly esteemed flavours of the gourmet and to aromatic foliage generally. Not a few members of this family have been singled out in preceding chapters for their visible qualities. The ever-loved lavender, the remembrance of rosemary with its nutmeg-like aroma, *Perovskia* of sage-like odour and the sages themselves, *Salvia officinalis* and its cultivars, are all shrubs worthy of a place for this and other reasons. We have considered the balm, *Melissa officinalis* and its golden counterpart, both of lemon tang, as also is *Thymus* x *citriodorus*, to which can be added *T. herba-barona* with a definite reminder of caraway and others of prostrate form sited where the occasional foot will stray.

We have accepted the visual value of the great hoary, aromatic leaves of the clary, *Salvia sclarea*, of the golden marjoram, *Origanum vulgare* 'Aureum' and the grey, strongly-scented foliage and long-flowering qualities of *Nepeta* x *faassenii* and 'Six Hills Giant'. Also in the flower border we can plant the bergamot, *Monarda didyma*, and its several cultivars as much for the pervading fragrance of foliage as for the flowers. By comparison *Calamintha grandiflora* is a mere dwarf but it too has redolent foliage to add to the small, but pretty rose-pink flowers.

The hyssop, *Hyssopus officinalis*, is a useful neat dwarf shrub with small, dark-green aromatic leaves and could more often be planted for ground cover in sunny, well-drained spots. In contrast the bastard or honey balm, *Melittis melissophyllum*, likes a cool and shady part of the garden or the woodland where the pleasant fragrance of its wrinkled, hairy leaves, which acquire a broad, purple, marginal band as they age, adds to the charm of its rosy-purple and white hooded flowers.

The mints, *Mentha*, are notedly aromatic but the majority have no outstanding attributes as garden plants and many are inclined to be rampageous through their underground rhizomes. The variegated apple mint, *M. rotundifolia* 'Variegata', as we have noted, is most desirable for foliar colour to clothe the ground. It is definitely mint scented with just a hint of apple to justify its common name. The Corsican mint, *M. requienii* and the penny-royal, *M. pulegium*, are mere carpeters for use in paving and places where they will occasionally be trodden on to release their peppermint odour.

There are others in this great race but we now turn to the family which makes perhaps the greatest contribution of all to our popular garden flowers and has numerous members with charmingly aromatic foliage.

Some Aromatic Composites

The feathery foliage of southernwood or lad's love, *Artemisia abrotanum*, is strongly but pleasantly pungent when bruised and a similar odour pervades the leaves of *A. ludoviciana* and others we have extolled for their silvery foliage. The culti-vated wormwood, *A. lactiflora*, has perhaps a little less pleasing

scent but, in its own right, is a most valuable late flowering
herbaceous plant. *Achillea* 'Moonshine' includes aroma with
its silvery foliage and lemon flower charms, and the forms of
A. filipendulina (*A. eupatorium*) with great golden plates of
flowers are equally as odoriferous. Indeed, this can be said
of practically all the species and forms of these two genera
commonly found in gardens.

The tansy, *Chrysanthemum vulgare*, and *C. argenteum*, both
formerly *Tanacetum*, the cultivated forms of the feverfew,
C. parthenium (*Matricaria eximia*) and *Calendula* grown for
bedding purposes all have their strong characteristic odours.
Much foliage aroma is indescribable or at least is peculiar to
the particular plant and cannot be likened to anything else.
This, however, is not the case with *Helichrysum angustifolium*
with attractive silvery-grey foliage smelling most decidedly of
curry.

For low ground cover, or even to make a lawn in appropriate
surrounds, the chamomile, *Chamaemelum nobile* (*Anthemis
nobilis*), is often lauded. For a lawn the dwarf non-flowering
clone 'Treneague' is to be preferred but, for all the fascination
of something other than grass and a clinging aroma to go with
it, one should be careful to restrict such a lawn to a manage-
able size, regarding it as a small seductive luxury for it will
not in itself completely and indefinitely maintain an upper
hand over coarse grass and other trespassers. I often think
that perhaps the most successful way to have a fragrant lawn
would be to try to emulate the close sward of coastal plateaus
and moorlands where the common thyme, *Thymus vulgaris*,
infiltrates through the fine-leaved grasses and induce this and
lawn grasses to intermingle as in nature, even if it did mean
less close cutting.

Scented-leaved Pelargoniums

I doubt if any other individual genus provides such a diversity
of foliage aromas, the majority highly acceptable, a few rather

repugnant. Equally diverse in the group is size and form of foliage, from tiny, thumb-nail leaves to those which the hand can barely cover, some uniform and entire, others with varying degrees of laciniation, to the pungent *Pelargonium denticulatum* 'Filicifolium' with finely divided fern-like leaves.

Unfortunately the group is not hardy, few have flowers of any class and their value is confined to their foliage, the highlight being scent when touched or bruised. For all their other limitations they are well worthy of a place in the summer garden, in the more formal parts adjacent to buildings, paved paths and the like, planted in tubs or urns well within touch and visually livened up with suitable associating flowers. Always, of course, they will charm within the precincts of greenhouse or conservatory.

Perhaps the most useful for general purposes is the lemon-scented *P. crispum* 'Variegatum' which has previously been mentioned as a worthy specimen foliage plant to associate with summer bedding. 'Clorinda' with unmistakably rose-scented foliage probably has the largest flowers and has a strong, somewhat-rambling habit which can be utilised for draping elevated receptacles or for covering a greenhouse wall.

One of the dwarfest, also rose-scented, is 'Little Gem' which has a larger counterpart in 'Attar of Roses'. 'Lady Plymouth' too has similar aromatic qualities. *P. x fragrans* smells strongly of nutmeg and is of useful dwarf grey-green form. There is also more than a hint of nutmeg in the leaves of 'Lady Mary' when bruised.

'Prince of Orange', as one would expect, provides a reminder of orange while *P. x nervosum* is lime-scented and 'Mabel Grey' more generally citrus. 'Old Spice' does not appear to be quite aptly named for it is more reminiscent of apples. 'Joy Lucille' and *P. tomentosum* are definitely peppermint-scented, 'Toronto' indicates ginger while 'Endsleigh' is quite markedly peppery. 'Camphor Rose' emits a camphor-like odour and *P. abrotanifolium* not only has much divided foliage but also the strong pungency of southernwood, *Artemisia abrotanum*.

In both shape and in the odour released, when their leaves are crushed, the members of the ivy-leaved group of *Pelargonium* can also be associated with that quite dissimilar plant the ivy, to provide one of the strange similitudes between quite unrelated plants. These pelargoniums are, of course, planted primarily for their flowers and a habit which can be utilised for trailing or for training upright in flower beds or for indoor or outdoor receptacles.

More Aromatic Plants

Culinary and medicinal herbs are again to the fore. Selecting only those which have something to please the visual as well as the nasal sense, there is sweet cicely, *Myrrhis odorata*, aniseed-scented, and fennel, *Foeniculum vulgare*, with its own particular brand of fragrance, both already with commendation for finely-divided foliage. Dill, *Anethum graveolens*, also has fern-like foliage and characteristic odour and is worthy of inclusion for these desirable traits even if its flowers have no real ornamental value.

The rue, *Ruta graveolens*, generally represented in gardens by 'Jackman's Blue' and occasionally also by 'Variegata' for foliage form and colour, is extremely pungent when bruised and has medicinal properties beneficial to both humans and poultry. The winter-green, *Gaultheria procumbens*, whose dark, shining leaves are unmistakenly redolent of the still-used medicinal oil or ointment, is a dwarf but dense carpeter for shady areas in lime-free soil and one that is by no means dismayed if this gets on the dry side when the tree leaf canopy is complete. It is also pretty with its pinkish-white bells of flowers followed by bright red berries, both often in existence at the same time.

Outside the culinary and medicinal range the bug-bane,

Cimicifuga, derives its name from the leaves which, *C. europaea*
(*C. foetida*) in particular, in Siberia are used to drive away
bugs. Thus we are hardly likely to seek it for any aroma its
leaves may possess but we can with profit plant *C. europaea
intermedia*, *C. dahurica* and especially *C. racemosa* for their
divided leaves and for their inviting long, closely packed,
upright racemes of white flowers in July and August. Semi-
shade is more acceptable to them than full sun.

Dictamnus albus (*D. fraxinella*) is variously called the
burning bush, dittany and fraxinella and is a worthwhile
occupant of any herbaceous border for its flowering qualities.
The leaves and stems are fragrant with lemon when brushed,
stronger and more like balsam when crushed, from a volatile
oil which is released, particularly on a hot day when a light
applied to the base of the inflorescence will momentarily
ignite without damage to the flowers. Thus burning bush is
the more appropriate of its common names.

It is unusual to find in a genus like *Primula*, noted for a
wealth of floral beauty, one species which adds scented foliage
to its attractions. This is *P. anisodora*, one of the less common
species whose purplish-wine coloured flowers, although
quite pleasing, cannot quite compete for spectacular effect
with other extremely floriferous and colourful members of the
candelabra group but virtually stands alone for its pleasantly
aromatic foliage.

Redolent Trees and Shrubs

Most woody genera with aromatic foliage release their
varying odours only when their leaves are crushed. We have
enjoyed the resinous fragrance of the conifers in a preceding
chapter but there are others which do cast their aromas on
the still air. Perhaps the most pervading are the balsam
poplars, although the fragrance arises mainly from the gummy
bud scales and is most pronounced in the early spring when
the buds are swelling. There is, however, more than a

hint of this seductive balsamic odour in the leaves themselves and throughout the whole of the year the trees will proclaim themselves at some little distance, to me providing an atmosphere that is unequalled by anything else. They are, unfortunately, of extremely vigorous growth, suited to the broader landscape only but I would tuck into some corner a young *Populus trichocarpa* or *P. candicans* and keep it to bushy proportions by stooling it down annually, leaving this operation as late in the winter as possible so as not to miss the zenith period. And as often as necessary I would insert a few, hardwood cuttings to provide a replacement when my bush got too old and tortured.

As an alternative *P. simonii* makes a smaller, more compact and rather more graceful tree of pyramidal habit, with pendulous branchlets, angled stems and small, shining, bright-green leaves with reddish petioles.

If we have no place for a walnut, *Juglans regia*, in the garden we can at least appreciate the sweet clinging fragrance of its leaves and stems, and when we are able to succeed in the open with *Eucalyptus gunnii* we shall prize it as much for the odour of its crushed leaves as their glaucous-grey hue, provided these are within reach on this fast, tall-growing subject. There can, of course, always be the one deliberately kept shrubby to provide cut foliage and enjoy at close quarters.

The Amur cork tree, *Phellodendron amurense*, really should have had its place among those with outstanding pinnate foliage. Aromatic when crushed, in appearance the tree is not unlike the tree of heaven, *Ailanthus altissima*, but, at 30-40ft, is little more than half its ultimate height and altogether more acceptable for the smaller garden.

The sweet bay, *Laurus nobilis*, has long been prized for its fragrant leaves still used for flavouring. Its evergreen ornamental value is such that in addition to being grown more often as a large bush than the bushy tree it will attain, it has also been used for hedgemaking and for formal clipped standards and pyramids in tubs. A severe winter may well leave it completely brown but generally the damage is superficial and new leaves duly emerge. This susceptibility makes it unwise to attempt too much with it in districts where winter winds blow strong and bitter.

Of all the plants which emit mild to strong hints of lemon from their leaves there is none quite so powerfully reminiscent as the lemon-scented verbena, *Aloysia triphylla* (*Lippia citriodora*). Unfortunately this semi-hardy small tree or large shrub succeeds outside only when planted against a south wall in the most favoured parts and usually has to be regaled in the hospitality of greenhouse or conservatory.

The Mexican orange flower, *Choisya ternata*, may occasionally be browned under full exposure and is a shrub prized chiefly for its deliciously fragrant flowers. It has, however, all the year round qualities of shining, bright-green foliage which is pungent, but not unpleasantly so, when crushed.

The common myrtle, *Myrtus communis*, is another good evergreen prolific with fragrant, white flowers but one for the milder parts only. The pleasant odour of its leaves when crushed brings back memories to which I cannot put a name but I have seen the scent described as a mixture of bayberry and sassafras.

The resinous scent of the leaves and stems of *Myrica gale* is wafted into the air and can be enjoyed on many a British moorland but seldom within the precincts of a garden where, if the soil is acid, a few ought occasionally to be planted for this quality alone. The aromatic Labrador tea, *Ledum groenlandicum* (*L. latifolium*) also requires similar soil conditions, is low-growing and evergreen and a very hardy, flowering shrub of considerable appeal although not widely grown.

I doubt if anyone would plant elders for the rather repugnant acrid odour of their leaves although those with golden foliage will have another value. *Skimmia laureola* is a humble evergreen, over-shadowed by *S. japonica* and others and the strong pungency of its crushed leaves may not warrant a place in the garden. On the other hand, those of *S. japonica* are milder with a pleasant hint of grapefruit. *Escallonia illinita* and *E. viscosa* enjoy no real popularity—perhaps it is the more than fanciful suggestion of a pigsty when the leaves are bruised. The ivies too are acrid but they can be accorded full marks in more than one direction and sphere.

With a generic name which stands for allurement one can be sure that this is a side reference to the strong aniseed-like perfume emitted from the bruised leaves of *Illicium*, a genus with a lot to commend it but one which has not achieved widespread fame, probably because there are reservations about the hardiness of even the toughest, *I. anisatum*. But here again, if foliage conscious and circumstances permit, the odd shrub will undoubtedly introduce its own brand of charm to a warm corner of the garden.

The sun roses, among the finest and most floriferous of flowering shrubs, cannot be grown without some fear of damage or loss except where the winters are generally reasonably kind, the soil is well drained and the position sunny. *C.* x *cyprius* is, however, reasonably tough although not the hardiest, an honour which probably goes to one of its parents, *C. laurifolius*. Apart from its crowning glory of large white flowers with crimson blotches at the base of the petals there is the resinous fragrance of the leaves and stems to also enchant.

The sweet briar, *Rosa rubiginosa* (*R. eglanteria*) is one of the wild roses worthy of a place in a species collection for its single pink flowers and red hips but it is most prized as an aromatic hedge and effective barrier, the fruity fragrance of its leaves being most discernible after a shower of rain or in the cool moistness of the early morning or late evening. The Penzance briars, to which *R. rubiginosa* has contributed a parental share, have perhaps a stronger, if not more generally pleasing, foliar perfume with greater floral beauty.

Those who enjoy, frost and snow permitting, the blooms of the earliest flowering of all rhododendrons, *R. dauricum,* which often commence to open in January will, during the summer, also be regaled by the sweet perfume of the leaves which floats through the air on a hot summer's day. I, for one, cannot walk through a planting of azaleas, deciduous or evergreen, without reviving memories of my journeyman days when the overall smell of the plants, not their flowers, always gripped me and, perhaps quite mistakenly, reminded me of rabbits. Not that it is unpleasant in any way but, although my nose often plays tricks and relays likenesses which my brain cannot always identify, I always had a soft spot in my heart for rabbits, at least as pets. Be that as it may, much of the charm of a garden lies in the things the eye cannot see, elusive scents and aromas which bring back memories.

It requires a connoisseur of fragrance rather than a confirmed horticulturist like myself to distinguish and describe, in terms outside my normal vocabulary, the fascination of plant scents. What I have written does no more than draw attention to another engrossing side of this study of foliage, its place and possibilities in the garden.

CHAPTER ELEVEN

Autumnal Glory

So FAR AS plant life is concerned no season of the year is dull and without some glory but for sheer panoramic beauty the popular vote lies between spring and autumn. How many would say with certainty that they prefer one or the other? The spring is the harbinger of summer splendour to follow, the autumn foretells the approach of winter and in its somewhat briefer dying fling closes the chapter on another growing season with perhaps even more resplendent tones of a different kind. And it is, of course, in the autumn that foliage holds sway as flowers fade into insignificance but, strangely, the thought of planting for the season when foliage really asserts itself is too often lost in providing for the spring and summer months.

Without necessarily implying that this thought should be uppermost in our minds when selecting trees and shrubs for the landscape and garden, other things being equal and adequate to meet the needs at other times of the year preference should, wherever possible, be given to those which terminate a season of usefulness with ephemeral beauty, and there are plenty of dual purpose subjects which do just that. Thought also should be given to their placing so that their autumn colour is displayed to the best effect with others also draped in dying robes.

The Glorious Acers

No genus contributes more from the ordinary field maple, *Acer campestre*, to the vividly coloured Japanese maples. The Norway maple, *A. platanoides*, is a blaze of gold, as is *A. cappadocicum* (*A. laetum*), and its cultivars, while the red or Canadian maple, *A. rubrum*, is resplendent in scarlet and red. These species may be too widespreading for the smaller garden and here there may be possibilities with the 'tailored' Scanlon introductions like *A. platanoides* 'Olmsted' and *A. rubrum* 'Scanlon' which are much narrower in outline. I know that by some the mere description of 'tailored' is viewed with a degree of scepticism as are many of the dwarfer, more formal trees, but who can deny that where the space is confined such types come into their own even if they are of dubious value for the wider vista. Here there may ultimately be a place for the taller Scanlon maples of less regular outline like the 'Charles F. Irish' and 'Cleveland' forms of the Norway maple. The broader, autumn landscape would surely benefit by a few more of this type rather than a surfeit of the common sycamore which, at the fall, has so little of distinction to offer.

There is rich autumn colour to be found among the snake bark maples to add to their attractive striated bark and other virtues. *A. grosseri hersii* (*A. hersii*) turns a brilliant red and *A. pensylvanicum* to bright gold; *A. capillipes* is shot with orange-red and yellow and made all the more colourful by the long racemes of key-like fruits of straw-yellow tint, while *A. cissifolium* goes off in shades of red and yellow.

A. nikoense is an acer of small to medium stature which terminates its season in startling shades of rosy-scarlet and gold, while even the bark of the paperbark maple, *A. griseum*, ceases to be the first to catch the eye when this tree puts on its autumnal coat of brilliant, deep-red foliage.

To dwell upon the glories of the Japanese maples would take too long and be superfluous for they do not lack acclaim. *A. palmatum* passes out in varying brilliant shades from gold to bronzy-red and rich scarlet. *A.p.* 'Osakazuki' in fiery scarlet is probably the most brilliant of all and in complete contrast the small dainty foliage of the dwarfer, more bushy 'Senkaki' turns to soft yellow through which the coral-red of the shoots and younger branches gleams. The dainty much divided foliage of *dissectum* and its forms changes to golden-bronze and coppery-red.

A. japonicum, also from Japan, takes its place with *A. palmatum* and here 'Vitifolium' is an outstanding performer when its outer leaves turn to brilliant red and are seated against those in more inner positions which, denied some of the light, may not pass beyond the bronzy-yellow shade.

With these Japanese maples the enchantment is not just sheer colour en masse but the variation in the predominantly red and yellow tones and in their contrast, when planted in colonies, with those bushes which are tardy to call it a day and persist in remaining green as long as possible.

Mountain Ashes and other Sorbus

As with the maples, to go the full round would take too much space so we briefly pause on the glories of the upright *Sorbus americana*, the spreading *S. scalaris*, the very compact *S. commixta*, *S. aucuparia* and most of its forms and pick out the popular *S. discolor* for its outstandingly rich, plum-red foliage. I refer, of course, to the species in common circulation under this name although it is not the true *S. discolor*, which is white-fruited. With stronger and more spreading branches *S. sargentiana* becomes a fiery red while, for a complete change *S. aucuparia* 'Beissneri' turns an attractive straw-yellow shade in keeping with the coppery tone of its trunk and main branches which characterise this cultivar. But I think my favourite in the pinnate-leaved mountain ash section of *Sorbus* is 'Joseph Rock' of rich, autumnal red against which the golden fruits form a picture to live in the memory. With its erect, compact habit this should be an ideal tree for the smaller garden or narrow street.

In the Micromeles and Aria sections with simple leaves there is, perhaps, a little less vivacity to support the gold of the whitebeam, *S. aria*, but far more use could be made of *S. alnifolia* which makes a comparatively small, fairly-erect tree and has neat foliage which turns to golden-bronze. To tone down the sheer brilliance of its associates generally *S. megalocarpa* changes its large, deep green leaves to rich purplish-bronze, and the nut-brown of *S.* 'Mitchellii' is made all the more interesting by the gradually curling margins of the leaves to more fully reveal the white tomentose under-surface, now becoming rather off-white with age.

More Resplendent Trees

Which is the prince of these? Possibly the sweet gum, *Liquidambar styraciflua*, a magnificent tree at all times and one which should be much more widely planted in gardens, on housing estates and alóngside roads for its habit and summer foliage alone. In the autumn it is magnificent in shades of crimson provided it is not hemmed in by other trees and bereft of full sunlight. Or it could be the tulip tree, *Liriodendron tulipifera*, contrasting with bright gold, or the broad cone of the tupelo, *Nyssa sylvatica*, in shades between yellow and scarlet according to aspect.

Certainly some of the oaks are challengers, either the rich, vinous red of the pin oak, *Quercus palustris*, the russetty-scarlet of the scarlet oak, *Q. coccinea*, or the deep red-brown of the larger leaves of the red oak, *Q. rubra* (*Q. borealis maxima*). Among deciduous conifers there is the rich bronze of *Taxodium distichum* and the more chestnut-brown of *T. ascendens* by the waterside, the clear yellow of the maidenhair tree, *Ginkgo biloba*, and the feathery blend of tawny-gold and rose of *Metasequoia glyptostroboides*.

The poplars are not particularly noted for autumn effect but one, the white poplar, *Populus alba*, does compel admiration when the upper surfaces of its leaves, having turned to gold, are competing for attention with the still, white undersurfaces being exposed as the leaves ripple in the breeze.

While the common ash, *Fraxinus excelsior*, will occasionally deign to lose its foliage in good, yellow tones, more especially young vigorous trees, it all too frequently fails to go down with really flying colours, but this cannot be said of the much dwarfer slower growing form 'Aurea', always attractive with its yellowish-green shoots and branches and leaves invariably turning to clear yellow in autumn. In contrast *F. oxycarpa* 'Raywood' turns to luminous purple hues, a welcome annual phase in the life of a moderately sized tree of graceful outline now becoming much in demand for housing estate planting.

Popular also for such purposes and one of the comparatively few ornamental crabs bedecked in the autumn, *Malus tschonoskii* starts going to rest with shades of purplish-bronze which spread and brighten to rich red and finally pale to orange-scarlet as the leaves begin to fall. It is also one of the few which are distinctly pyramidal in habit, tending to retain a single leader longer than most deciduous trees and although not one of the finest in flower and fruit, for form and autumn colour it virtually stands alone.

Among the smaller ornamental trees *Prunus sargentii* is quite supreme. One of the first of all trees to acknowledge the end of the summer it terminates in brilliant shades of deep red with orange to close a chapter which commenced in March with. leafless branches wreathed with rich, pink flowers followed by bronzy, young leaves. By comparison the autumn tints of the much planted Japanese cherries tend to be rather insignificant although some cultivars in some soils and seasons do contribute their share without seriously challenging the

supremacy of *sargentii*. For really good support we are most
likely to be well served by some of the hybrid cherries,
P. x *hillieri* 'Spire', *P.* x *schmittii*, 'Pandora', 'Kursar' and
'Umineko'. All are small upright trees eminently suitable for
the less capacious garden and all very early in flower and
colourful in the autumn.

Two lesser-known cherries are particularly conspicuous at
this season, the Chinese hill cherry, *P. serrulata hupehensis*, in
rich vinous red coat and *P.* 'Hilling's Weeping' in orange-
scarlet and gold made all the more outstanding by its very
pronounced weeping habit, many of the branches descending
quite perpendicularly with no attempt to arch over first.

The amelanchiers, *A. laevis* (of gardens) and *A.* x *grandiflora*,
are really magnificent whether they are treated as small trees
or kept to shrubby status. *Crataegus prunifolia* forms a dwarf,
round-headed tree with dark green, shiny leaves which turn
to rich crimson shades to accompany its large, persistent
scarlet haws.

Those who like the fine pinnate foliage of the false acacia,
Robinia pseudacacia, and have room for a tree ultimately
reaching considerable dimensions, will also find a place for
the honey locust, *Gleditsia triacanthos*, for its elegant foliage
which turns to bright yellow in autumn and also in the hope
of it occasionally setting a few of its 12-18in long brown seed
pods. They will also plant *Pterocarya fraxinifolia* (*P. caucasica*)
for similar foliage effect but if their room is limited they
will be content and very well served by the autumn gold of
Koelreuteria paniculata which has been eulogised elsewhere in
this book.

So has *Cercidiphyllum japonicum*, magnificent in shades of red
and yellow and, in similar vein, *Parrotia persica*, more often
seen as a large, spreading shrub, has claims to be among the
first half dozen colourful at this season.

We see and hear too little about the stewartias (stuartias).
Perhaps it is because they are not easy to obtain and establish

and they do like a lime-free soil, some shade and shelter from neighbouring trees. White flowers over a fairly long period in July and August make them quite valuable and at all times their thinly-flaking bark revealing the lighter inner bark in irregular patches of varying shades according to the length of exposure, attracts attention. In the autumn *S. pseudocamellia* in particular is resplendent with its dying foliage in shades of scarlet to crimson, green-edged for a while against the inner, sun-starved leaves content to turn to yellow and bronze.

Oxydendroum arboreum has similar requisites and, likewise, is all too rare. As a small tree or large shrub it forms a unique and enchanting spectacle in autumn when the leaves turn to a deep maroon-red percolated with yellow and the whole surmounted by the feathery haze of the remains of the slender racemes of flowers produced in open, arching tufts at the ends of the shoots.

Rhus typhina and its cultivar 'Laciniata' are among the first to bedeck themselves in brilliant scarlet and orange and draw all eyes before the acers are properly under way but may still be competing for credit when the full flush of autumn colour is building up. Their characteristic spreading form and pinnate leaves ensure them remaining real eye catchers. Like the *Rhus*, *Cornus florida* and *C. kousa* hover between large shrubs and small bushy trees and it is difficult to decide whether their finest hour is the May and June 'floral' display of white bracts or the richness of their rosy-red autumnal dress.

Cladrastis lutea, a very fine, small tree with pendent panicles of white flowers in June, ends the season with rich golden foliage. It should be more widely planted as should *Photinia villosa* (*P. variabilis*), another small tree or large shrub with white flowers in May and attractive red fruits and, in particular, dying foliage of bright scarlet and gold which is by no means outshone by the plethora of such colours when October is passing and early frosts speed up the transition from the green of summer.

Rhus typhina 'Laciniata': at its peak in autumn dress of orange and scarlet.

With the scintillating mannequins in autumnal dress there is the backcloth in depth of the gold, russet, brown and reddish-bronze of indigenous countryside trees like the common and durmast oaks, the horsechestnut, the common beech and the silver birch. This annual panoramic display is there for all to see and is not tucked away in gardens, making a contribution to the autumn scene far greater than the vivacity of the few.

Autumnal Shrubs

Many of the popular deciduous flowering shrubs such as *Philadelphus*, *Weigela*, *Deutzia*, *Forsythia* and *Buddleia* make little or very half-hearted attempts to fade out gracefully. Together with the evergreen kinds whose solidity is most appreciated after leaf fall, shrub borders in autumn are liable to have dull patches unless some advantage is taken of those which become alive at that season with foliage and/or fruits.

Where the deciduous azaleas abound there will be colour in abundance in varying shades of red through to solid purplish-maroon and their value at this season is almost as great as their contribution to the spring scene. But azaleas are subjects for the woodland, for grouping with their evergreen cousins in more natural surrounds rather than performing a supporting role with flower and foliage in the mixed shrub border, although they can often be employed with advantage in this way when it is not possible to give them the setting and conditions most befitting to them.

Always, of course, there is the question of neutral to acid soil containing a plentiful supply of humus, a prerequisite also of *Fothergilla major* and *F. monticola*, probably the finest of all autumn-foliaged shrubs. These are now considered to be the same species with *F. major* given the precedent. Under whatever name they are grown there is likely to be considerable variation in the autumn tints, in a particular season and from year to year. It may in the main be rich gold or it may be more transitional, passing from gold to brilliant scarlet and rich deep red, all colours being present for a spell with here and there a shoot with purplish-red leaves, ending the growing season which began in spring with a display of bottle-brush flowers consisting mainly of bosses of long-stalked white stamens with conspicuous yellow anthers.

Another subject for a lime-free soil, *Enkianthus campanulatus* is aflame with red and gold after it has charmed in the spring with its small creamy-yellow, bell-shaped flowers so exquisitely

tipped and chequered with bronzy-red. Nowhere have I seen
it quite so richly coloured deep wine-red in autumn than in
my own garden where one bush was planted in a pocket of
peaty soil surrounded by the sticky yellow clay I have to
wrestle with. One hopes it will not go into reverse when its
roots start to penetrate this not too inviting medium.

The witch hazels, *Hamamelis*, so valuable for their fragrant
flowers on the leafless branches in the early part of the year,
become resplendent with gold. So too does *Hydrangea
paniculata* 'Grandiflora' set off by the remains of the large
panicles of flowers which by then have turned from white to
a pinkish-green.

The small leaves on the arching branches of *Spiraea prunifolia*
change to rich orange and red, the Venetian sumach, *Cotinus
coggyria* (*Rhus cotinus*) likewise is aflame while its purple-
leaved cultivars, like other trees and shrubs of this colour,
tend to lose some of their normal depth of tone and become
lighter, brighter and more buoyant before they fall.

Many viburnums pass out in extra deep tones, from the
pink to reddish-crimson of the ordinary guelder rose, *V.
opulus*, of the hedgerows and its cultivars to the deeper
crimson of *V. plicatum* whose cultivar 'Grandiflorum' is usually
particularly fine. The leaves of *V. setigerum* (*V. theiferum*) end
the season in even deeper wine-purple tones than they began,
but the deepest of all are those of *V. furcatum*, larger than the
majority and really maroon-purple, dull in comparison to the
vivid scarlets and golds which prevail but invaluable for
contrast and for their deep solidity.

To introduce further change into the kaleidoscope of
colour there is nothing more refreshing than the callicarpas
where hues of mauve with rose and pink are in keeping with
the unusual violet berries which wreathe the branches and
also combine admirably with the reds, russets and golds
around. *C. bodinieri giraldii* (*C. giraldiana*) and *C. dichotoma*
(*C. koreana*) are the two most commonly seen, both similar

in flower and fruit but the latter the dwarfer and more compact of the two.

The common dogwood, *Cornus alba*, turns to deep plum-crimson but in gardens is usually represented by forms with more richly coloured red stems or with variegated foliage. When autumn arrives deep rose-red begins to creep in from the margins of the golden-variegated leaves of 'Gouchaltii' and gradually pervades the whole, becoming quite delightful for a brief spell preceding leaf fall. We should also appreciate the attempts of some of the hypericums to assume an autumn mantle, if not one that stands out in the mass of colour around. With the well-known *H. patulum henryi*—now rather lost in a maze of names such as *beanii*, *forrestii* and *pseudohenryi*, and rather overshadowed as a flowering shrub by hybrids like 'Hidcote'—rich, glowing red creeps into the older leaves until the laminas are completely coloured with the mid ribs and main veins picked out in orange, the whole surmounted by the still green younger leaves.

The barberries with flowers and foliage, and spiny habit to deter trespassers where such protection is needed, do sterling work at all seasons. In the autumn the deciduous species are highly prized for their prolific and colourful berries and many have attendant, equally as colourful, foliage. *Berberis thunbergii* is superb, *wilsoniae*, *yunnanensis*, *aggregata*, x *rubrostilla* and their hybrids are other popular sorts alive with colour of leaf and fruit, but I think one of the finest for such foliage is *sieboldii*, not quite so widely planted as the others but deserving of equal popularity for its intense scarlet alone.

On that note we turn to a few shrubs where autumn value is so outstanding that they must be included in a collection of any size, even if at other seasons their contribution is not great. In this respect the deciduous *Euonymus* are pre-eminent. To see a bush of *E. alatus* ablaze with rosy-red, in overall hue so different from the majority of its neighbours, is a never-to-be forgotten sight, as is *E. latifolius* from the early days of rosy-red

spreading in with the veins outlined in yellow until it becomes
one warm mass further enlivened by the profusion of similarly-
coloured fruits splitting open to reveal the orange seed coats.
The common spindle, *E. europaeus*, cannot be denied although,
because it has the capacity to become a small tree, may not
be allowed to occupy the space in the smaller garden or more
cultivated parts.

If *Disanthus cercidifolius* has no outstanding merit when in
flower in October this matters little for that is the time when
the foliage turns to a rich, vinous purple to match the tempo
of the season.

The chokeberries, *Aronia*, are under-estimated shrubs.
They are of medium size only and quite attractive in May with
small corymbs of white flowers but it is the autumn when they
excel with exceptionally-brilliant red dying foliage which is
not just a few days 'flash in the pan'. *A. arbutifolia* and its
more upright form 'Erecta' have persistent red berries, with
A. melanocarpa they are black and not quite so showy but this
has a form, 'Brilliant' which has claims to be the most vivid
of all with autumnal coloration.

Finally, from chokeberries to bilberries, whortleberries,
huckleberries, cranberries and blueberries, to the genus
Vaccinium which produces these fruits to satisfy the inner man,
but has never achieved real fame for its ornamental value.
Perhaps this is because its best offerings are fruits and autumn
foliage, and also that an acid, fairly-moist soil is required.
Where such conditions prevail there is no dearth of more
floriferous and showy subjects to support rhododendrons and
heaths and no place for the less conspicuous *Vaccinium*. In the
fall, however, it comes to the fore on mountain and moorland
and in woodlands. In gardens we ought at least occasionally to
plant, in the interests of autumn days, the odd bush of, say,
V. corymbosum or one of its cultivars for the brilliance of the
orange-scarlet and bronze with yellow of their foliage.

Glorious Climbers

One must give pride of place to the spectacular self-clinging Virginian creepers, to use the common name by which they are best known. Now sorted out, the one with palmate leaves which has masqueraded for so long as the Virginian creeper should, evidently, now be called the Boston ivy, *Parthenocissus tricuspidata* (*Vitis inconstans*) with its somewhat smaller leaved form 'Veitchii' and its improvement 'Beverley Brook'. This is probably the best for walls as it is rather better furnished with self-clinging pads than the true Virginian creeper, *P. quinquefolia*, which has leaves composed of usually five leaflets and is ideal in habit for scrambling up trees. Anxious to get into autumn plumage, their brilliant scarlet tones are usually the first indication that summer is on the way out. *P. henryana* is another admirable species for clothing a south or west wall.

Even this magnificence is likely to be surpassed by *Vitis coignetiae* with leaves up to a foot across passing through scarlet to rich crimson and very much more at home vigorously wending its way up a large tree than cramped for space on a house wall, although in these more confined quarters it will still be very spectacular. While other vines may suffer somewhat in comparison *V.* 'Brant' (often mis-spelt 'Brandt'), one of the most widely planted of the outdoor fruiting vines, is not completely outdone when its leaves change to deep red and purplish-crimson.

For golden tints there is none clearer than *Celastrus orbiculatus* (*C. articulatus*) although here the surest eye-catcher will be the accompanying fruits splitting open and turning back to expose the scarlet-arilled seeds. The self-clinging *Hydrangea petiolaris* (now relegated to a subspecies of *H. anomala*), so good for a shady wall, will terminate its season with soft, pale-yellow tones in such a situation.

There are other vines of *Vitis* or *Parthenocissus* classification which also do their best to bring added glory to the climbing shrubs but, these two genera apart, there is a dearth of autumn colour in the ranks and one would wish there was a little more displayed by the numerous and popular honeysuckles and *Clematis*. Among the non-climbing shrubs normally used for clothing fences and walls there are, likewise, few with good autumnal dress, but perhaps this is just as well with the galaxy of colour which is possible if we plant generally for all seasons.

Herbaceous Plants

Although trees and shrubs absolutely predominate in the autumn it would be wrong to overlook the comparatively modest contribution of the non-woody genera. By far the majority die down unsung but a few have a brief last fling before going to rest.

Alchemilla mollis turns to soft yellow, many of the hostas are bright with gold before the brown of death begins to curl in

Vitis coignettae: large leaves and magnificent autumn colour make this one of the finest of foliage vines.

from the leaf margins. *Helleborus niger* too will turn to gold and there is colour for a time in the yellow-brown fading leaves on the arching stems of *Smilacina racemosa* and the Solomon's seal, *Polygonatum multiflorum* and its more vigorous garden form *P. x hybridum*.

Peltiphyllum peltatum becomes shot with reddish-bronze which may also extend almost to the veins leaving them outlined in yellow. *Polygonum bistorta* 'Superbum' goes purplish-brown and many of the ornamental grasses and their flowering spikes dry up in straw-coloured shades. The royal fern, *Osmunda regalis*, passes through tawny-gold and chestnut-brown before acquiring a truly dead look and is supported by other ferns as if to compensate in gardens for the absence of the outlawed bracken.

The sub-shrubby *Ceratostigma plumbaginoides* turns to bronze and red before dying down and *Cornus canadensis* (by some now accorded and encumbered with the monotypic generic rank of *Chamaepericlymenum canadense*), begins to burnish its leaves with red, some of which may survive the whole winter. And in similar vein the evergreen leaves of bergenias, *Tellima*, *Tiarella*, *Galax* and others begin to prepare for the winter and more prominence in the next chapter.

CHAPTER TWELVE

Changing to Winter Garments

IT IS NOT SURPRISING that, with the approach of winter, the foliage of some evergreens tends to lose a little of the lustre of summer and becomes somewhat more solid without in any way appearing gloomy. Too few people plant for winter interest and effect; even fewer have regard to the extraordinary number of plants which tend to go gay at that season as if to rejoice and take full advantage of the shifting of the spotlight. The value of such plants is not always appreciated as much as it ought to be, for in some cases this is a second stint, having already done their main task of enhancing the beauty of the garden when all around is competition.

The invaluable Bergenias
Architectural in their foliage at all seasons and splendid ground coverers in sun or shade, quite enchanting with their flowers as soon as, or even before, spring dawns, when the first frosts of autumn are upon us the leaves of many of the species and cultivars begin to assume rich red to maroon tints. These gradually spread from the perimeters of the leaves inwards until, in many cases, the whole becomes a rich, heart-warming hue. Among the princes are *Bergenia purpurascens* (*B. delavayi*) with smaller, rather more ovate leaves than most species.

The hybrid 'Sunningdale' has a red reverse, 'Ballawley' turns reddish-bronze rather than maroon and is a little inclined to lose its leaves during a particularly severe spell, while among the others 'Profusion' and the quite dwarf 'Abendglut' ('Evening Glow') are worthy of special mention. Those who use bergenias as shade plants may not reap such a fine winter harvest and it is well worth ensuring that some of the best 'chameleons' are given a sunny position to enhance their winter coats.

Burnished Foliage

Absorption of the infra-red rays of the sun seems to be some prerequisite for this off-season gaiety. Strangely, most of the best displayers are plants which appreciate, or do not object to, some shade. *Mahonia aquifolium*, a shrub of infinite value for clothing shady places, when grown in full sun is appreciably more burnished with purplish-bronze in winter. It also produces its upright racemes of sweetly-scented flowers before all the blasts of winter have passed, then in early autumn bedecks itself with luscious black fruits which make a very passable 'blackcurrant type' jam and earn for it the popular name of Oregon grape. This multi-purpose shrub, so easy to grow, is always at its finest, in shape as well as in colour, when used with discretion as a source of cut foliage, or the longest growths are otherwise removed occasionally to keep it sturdy in growth and well furnished to the base. There is a form or hybrid called 'Moseri' which is quite delightful. Throughout the summer its younger foliage is well permeated with pinkish-red which becomes more pronounced as the days get shorter.

Among the ericaceous aristocrats *Leucothoe fontanesiana*, better known as *L. catesbaei*, has floral beauty of a different but most appealing kind. A first class evergreen at all seasons, its arching branches, graced in May and June with pendant white, lily-of-the-valley like flowers, never look better than

when water is not too far away. Then in winter the foliage
becomes burnished with bronze if the situation has not had
too much summer shade. Experimenting as I so often do with
different foliage to furnish dried flower and grass arrangements
I have found this subject preserves remarkably well when
impregnated with a glycerine solution as practised with beech
leaves. This accentuates the natural burnishing and the
arching sprays make most desirable material for the purpose.

Euonymus fortunei (E. radicans) 'Coloratus' makes a sprawling
low shrub which is extremely valuable where tall ground
cover is required in sun or shade. Its leaves assume rich tints
of brown and purple during the winter, stronger and much
more pronounced when growing in full sun.

Tints with Heathers

There are few races of plants which contribute as much
throughout the whole year with so little attention as the
heathers. In looking in a previous chapter at some of the ever-
increasing band of foliage cultivars I purposely omitted a few
which could well have received commendation there but the
gold reserves among the heaths are so rapidly expanding that
I feel that those which change from gold to copper and reddish-
bronze at the advent of the winter should be considered in
conjunction with the more pressing needs of that season. The
cultivars of the common ling, Calluna vulgaris, again predominate and of those which take on rich burnished tones in
winter I feel I like 'Blazeaway' slightly better than 'Robert
Chapman' as a foliage plant but during the flowering season
its lighter, mauve flowers, although rather more freely
produced, do not contrast quite so well with the then golden
foliage. There is really little to choose between them when
flowering is over and the foliage gradually changes to the
warm red tints of winter, literally glowing in the weakened
sunshine. My fancy is that 'Blazeaway' just has the edge but
some slight variation of soil or aspect could shift the balance

and it may well be that flowering will decide the issue—one hardly needs both unless a heather fanatic and a hoarder of the hundreds of first class cultivars now available. The newer 'Sir John Charrington' may yet challenge them both for foliage, with its crimson flowers an added incentive to give it preference.

There is another newcomer in 'Winter Chocolate' which undergoes several changes of raiment from red tips to the young spring growths, developing to green and orange and ageing to chocolate later in the season to justify its name. 'Cuprea' has naturally coppery foliage which deepens in intensity as winter gets under way. 'Sunset' turns from the gold of summer to a striking chestnut-red, 'Golden Feather' becomes more of a salmon-red and the closely packed mats of 'John F. Letts' literally glow with similar coloration. 'Multi-color' is probably the deepest colour of all at that season, burnishing to a red so deep that it almost becomes maroon.

Among the ericas winter garments are not as yet quite so much worn. _Erica cinerea_ 'Golden Drop', although its coppery-gold foliage changes to a most attractive russet-red, is a shy bloomer and not of the easiest culture. The winter-flowering heath, _E. carnea_, needs no coloured foliage among its ranks to set off the blooms at that season but I find the fleckings of darker bronze on the golden-bronze foliage of 'Ann Sparkes' singularly appealing and not at all competitive with the deep carmine flowers.

Climbers and Ground Coverers
Among climbing plants the winter-flowering, evergreen _Clematis calycina_ (_C. balearica_) has dark, glabrous-green, summer foliage which assumes bronzed tints in winter to give background to the creamy-white, nodding flowers which, delicately and attractively speckled with reddish-purple inter-nally belie the blasts of January and February if given the protection of a south wall and some shelter from strong winds.

Tellima grandiflora: a splendid ground coverer with foliage turning rich red in winter.

The golden reticulated leaves of *Lonicera japonica* 'Aureo-reticulata' become shot with red after a few hard frosts. The large leaved ivy, *Hedera canariensis* 'Variegata' ('Gloire de Marengo') gradually assumes its winter mantle as some of the green in the variegated leaves deepens to purplish-brown and a pink and red staining begins to permeate the silver, being more pronounced towards the edges, altogether quite a fascinating combination of colours.

Today's accent on ground cover, which one must applaud, and modern trends in floral arrangement have brought *Tellima grandiflora* out of obscurity. Happy alike in sun or shade it clothes the ground with its broad domes of foliage rather than by sidewards spread of creeping roots or stems which typify so many plants used for this purpose. Its rounded, bright-green leaves have character in summer, aided by the terminal racemes of creamy-green flowers on 2-2½ ft stems (pinkish in the form *purpurea*) which are a joy to the flower arranger. In the winter the foliage becomes a deep, burnished red what-ever the aspect where it is growing. This plant would make a delightful ground coat for many of the early flowering bulbs were it not that, like most clump-forming plants, although it will steadily increase in girth for a number of years without noticeably losing vigour, it does appreciate an occasional lifting, dividing and replanting. Most of the best naturalising bulbs are, of course, best left undisturbed indefinitely and seem to gain in vigour and effectiveness as they thicken out into colonies. The *Tellima* will, however, produce some charming effects in association with other winter foliage, silver and grey in particular.

One cannot fail to be entranced with the pretty frilled or fringed flowers of *Shortia* (*Schizocodon*) *soldanelloides*, *S. galaci-folia* and *S. uniflora* 'Grandiflora', all really beautiful plants for a moist, lime-free soil with plenty of humus in partial shade. Slowly they form a low carpet of rounded, shiny-green leaves which take on red tints during the winter. While some exposure to full summer sunshine will result in more vivid coloration later it must not be overdone for these plants must have a reasonable amount of diffused light when the sun is at its most powerful.

In the same family but a much larger plant, *Galax aphylla* is also a woodlander and a splendid ground coverer even in deep shade, producing its tapering erect racemes of white flowers in June. The large, rounded leaves during the summer are permeated with bronzy red from autumn until spring.

The foam flower, *Tiarella cordifolia*, fully justifies its popular name with a haze of white flowers in May and June on a low carpet of foliage which spreads steadily but not invasively and at the fall takes on tints of bronze and pink. Again this likes a cool, moist root run and partial shade but I find it rather more accommodating than *Shortia* and *Galax* in that it does not shy at my rather heavy clay soil, providing it has a reasonable start. With me it grows quite happily in a quite sunny position which brings out its best in winter. This is a more suitable companion than *Tellima* for small bulbs for as a mat former it can be kept growing quite vigorously and evenly, even in the centre, by carefully poking in an annual top dressing of leafy compost. If it becomes necessary to re-invigorate by lifting and replanting, provided the bulbs are planted a little deeper than usual, this operation can with a little care be done without unduly disturbing the bulbs. Snowdrops and *Crocus chrysanthus* 'Snow Bunting' look particularly well thrusting through the multi-coloured mat of winter foliage. The untidiness of the bulbs as they pass out of flower and concentrate on foliage growth and food storage for the following year before dying down is soon lost as the *Tiarella* clothes itself with its foamy mass of flowers.

There is always something of interest among the epimediums to make their common name of barrenwort appear a complete misnomer, but doubtless it has another meaning. As mentioned in a previous chapter, some are quite delightful for a time when

they unfurl their leaves and all provide a charming green
mantle during the summer months. Those that are evergreen
take on burnished autumnal and winter tints, none excelling
Epimedium x *versicolor*, its pale yellow flowered variant *sulphurea* and *E.* x *warleyense* with most attractive orange-red
flowers. Shade or part shade suits them best and they are not
miffy about soil provided it is not too impoverished.

   Arctostaphyllos uva-ursi is a tiny, ground-hugging ericaceous

Epimedium x *versicolor:* one of the best of the ground covering barrenworts for
burnished winter foliage.

native shrub with small, white-tinted, flowers which delights
in a peaty-acid root run and likes the sun just as well as partial
shade when it becomes burnished with purplish tones in
winter.

The polygonums are an incomprehensible race. They may
be pernicious annual weeds like knotgrass, *P. aviculare*, and
black bindweed, *P. convolvulus*, invasive sub-shrubs, rampant
perennial climbers like the Russian vine, *P. baldschuanicum*,
or quite delightful flowering plants for woodland, waterside
or rock garden. For winter foliage the mat forming *R. affine*,
whether it be the type or currently popular cultivars like
'Darjeeling Red' and 'Donald Lowndes', follows a quite invaluable late summer and autumn display of pink flowers with
an equally valuable winter coat of brown to red foliage. While
it is, perhaps, happiest in partial shade I do not hesitate to give
it more exposure to the sun to intensify this coloration for, in
my soil, I am ensured of the moist root run it likes, except
during extremely severe drought.

Many a small, humble plant incites my interest and admiration, for the hallmark of distinction and true value lies not
in looks alone but also in the service given to a garden. Such a
plant is *Linnaea borealis*, a tiny, creeping woodlander which
belies its humble appearance by producing the most exquisite
little flesh-pink flowers in pairs. But it is not this that concerns
us here, although it is of paramount importance to mention, if
only in passing, attractions other than foliage.

Linnaea must have a cool soil full of humus if it is to make a
really good carpet and assume its bronzy tints in winter to make
it perhaps even more valuable at that season than when it is
charming with flowers.

Beauty of Dead Leaves
He who, when autumn leaves have fallen and the foliage of
herbaceous plants has turned to brown or straw-coloured
remnants, sets out and religiously cuts back all dead annual

stems and foliage and cleans up and either burns or stacks the
fallen leaves of deciduous trees and shrubs has a tidy, but aw-
fully bare, garden for the whole of the winter. Moreover, he
is at cross purposes with nature for she does not remove the
natural protection of her plants, exposing the crowns to every
wintery blast and permitting frost unimpeded access to their
roots. Many a plant survives severe weather only because of
the protection afforded by the remains of the previous season's
growth whether it be still held aloft or has crumpled over the
crown of the plant.

What is more, a plant by its annual process of partial death
and decay returns to the earth much of that it has taken out.
The gardener may certainly replace it by manuring and
fertilising the more cultivated parts of his garden but seldom
is this extended to trees and shrubs. If their fallen leaves are
left they ultimately form a mulch of humus over the surface,
supplying nourishment, helping to keep the soil cool and
moist and stifling the germination of weed seeds. It may be
necessary to remove leaves from lawns, paths, rose and flower
beds and collect them when they have blown into corners,
but wherever possible they should be left, at least until the
winter is passing and plant life is on the move once more.

The stems and leaves of herbaceous plants should likewise be
left for as long as possible. They do, after all, remind one of
the summer that has passed and in the robes of death they do
add some colour and warmth to the garden. How pleasant are
the commons, woodlands and moors where the ubiquitous
bracken is growing in great tracts of chestnut brown in late
autumn, deepening and getting a little deader in colour as
winter progresses. How pleasant, warm and comforting are
hedges of beech and hornbeam, or young trees of these and
oaks, all of which have the strange capacity, when young or
when their natural upward growth is prohibited, of retaining
their dead leaves until the buds burst again.

The dead growth of some of the ornamental grasses has

considerable winter value. *Miscanthus sinensis* turns to light straw colour still surmounted by the silvery plumes of the dead flowering stems. Stipas and *Pennisetum alopecuroides* can be most ornamental while *Melica altissima* may have its dead blades interspersed with much that is still green for most of the winter. All this welcome colour is lost when the plants are sheared down.

It does pay, therefore, to study what is worth while leaving for as long as possible, be it dead foliage or the flowering remains, for it may have its own particular brand of beauty and, at least, the garden or landscape will not be as bare and cold, in fact as well as in outlook, if it is left until new verdure is imminent.

While it was never my intention to cover subjects other than those which are hardy or near so, or which can be grown outside to enhance the summer and winter garden, I cannot close without some reference to the wealth of foliage available to those who are able to provide the heat and moisture of warmer climes within the protection of a glasshouse. Those familiar with the tropics know full well the lushness and the marvellous pattern of colour, the delicate traceries in the leaves of plants in regions of heat and constant high atmospheric moisture. Crotons in their varied leaf shapes with marvellous combinations of colour, the papery brilliance of caladiums and the marbled majesty of *Anthurium warocqueanum* are way outside the scope of this book and the majority of people who will read it. But those who, in their homes, now enjoy and marvel at the leaf formations and etchings of marantas, peperomias and other tropical plants which of recent years have been made available for house culture, will have learnt to recognise that the character and the attraction of the open garden can depend just as much on foliage as on flowers. Give it its rightful place, use it with intent, value the tranquility and the balance it gives and the garden will never be a dull place, even when the flowers are gone.

Acknowledgements

My grateful thanks are due to Mr C. D. Brickell, Director of the Royal Horticultural Society's Garden, Wisley, for reading through the manuscript and bringing the nomenclature up-to-date in this age of many changes. I am also grateful to Elsa Megson and Messrs M. Clift, R. J. Corbin, E. L. Crowson, A. J. Huxley and H. Smith and to Suttons Seeds Ltd and John Waterer, Sons and Crisp Ltd who have provided me with photographs.

Index of Common Names of Plants

Index of Latin Names of Plants